THE LIVING ROOM SERIES

RUTH

loss, love & legacy

kelly minter

LifeWay Press®
Nashville, Tennessee

Published by LifeWay Press®
© 2009 • Kelly Minter
Seventh printing 2012

ISBN 978-1-4158-6693-1
Item 005189427

Dewey decimal classification: 222.35
Subject heading: BIBLE. O.T. RUTH \ CHRISTIAN LIFE \ FAITH

To order additional copies of this resource, write LifeWay Church Resources Customer Service; One LifeWay Plaza; Nashville, TN 37234-0113; FAX order to (615) 251-5933; call toll-free (800) 458-2772; e-mail *orderentry@lifeway.com;* order online at *www.lifeway.com;* or visit the LifeWay Christian Store serving you.

Printed in the United States of America

Adult Ministry Publishing
LifeWay Church Resources
One LifeWay Plaza
Nashville, TN 37234-0152

TABLE OF CONTENTS

RUTH: LOSS, LOVE & LEGACY

MEET THE AUTHOR
KELLY MINTER

KELLY MINTER IS AN AUTHOR, SPEAKER, SONGWRITER, AND SINGER.

SHE IS PASSIONATE ABOUT WOMEN DISCOVERING CHRIST THROUGH THE PAGES OF SCRIPTURE. SO WHETHER IT'S THROUGH A SONG, STUDY, OR SPOKEN WORD, KELLY'S DESIRE IS TO AUTHENTICALLY EXPRESS CHRIST TO THE WOMEN OF THIS GENERATION. IN A CULTURE WHERE SO MANY ARE HURTING AND BROKEN, SHE LOVES TO SHARE ABOUT THE HEALING AND STRENGTH OF CHRIST THROUGH THE BIBLE'S TRUTH.

Her first Bible study, *No Other Gods,* is the first installment of *The Living Room Series,* which helps women unveil the false gods in their lives for the ultimate purpose of discovering freedom in the one, true God. *Ruth: Loss, Love & Legacy* focuses on the inspiring story of Ruth presented in the same *LIving Room Series* format (studies can be done in any order).

Kelly writes extensively and speaks and leads worship at women's conferences, retreats, and events. She recently recorded *Loss, Love & Legacy* specifically written to complement this study. She also has a worship record entitled *Finer Day.* To view more of Kelly's music projects, books, studies, and calendar, visit *www.kellyminter.com.*

INTRODUCTION

I WAS SITTING WITH A FRIEND ACROSS A SMALL WOODEN TABLE IN ONE OF MY FAVORITE NASHVILLE CAFES, CHIN IN HAND, WHEN IN A WILTING TONE I EXPRESSED HOW MUCH I REALLY WANTED TO WRITE A BIBLE STUDY ON THE BOOK OF RUTH.

I'M FAIRLY CERTAIN WE WERE THE ONLY TWO IN THE RESTAURANT HAVING THIS CONVERSATION, THOUGH AT LEAST WE LOOKED LIKE EVERYONE ELSE WITH OUR NIFTY CHEESE PLATE. AFTER HAVING WRITTEN MY FIRST BIBLE STUDY *No Other Gods,* A TOPICAL STUDY ON CONFRONTING OUR MODERN-DAY IDOLS, I LONGED TO DELVE INTO A SPECIFIC BOOK AND LET SOMEONE ELSE'S STORY LEAD ME—PREFERABLY A WOMAN'S STORY IF POSSIBLE, AND MAYBE A WOMAN WHO KNEW BOTH SINGLE AND MARRIED LIFE, CHILDREN AND BARRENNESS, LOSS AND FULLNESS—THOUGH NOT TO APPEAR PICKY. I KNEW OF ONLY ONE PLACE TO TURN.

The Book of Ruth, nestled between Judges and 1 Samuel, is a short, four-chapter narrative that wraps together the human experience of loss, love, and legacy with the divine hope and sovereignty of a redeeming God. From its pages steps a wayfaring foreigner into the town of Bethlehem, amidst hardship and famine and tragedy, affecting the course of human history forever.

A widow turned wife, a servant turned heir, a childless foreigner turned mother, she was born in Moab but found her home in Israel. Ruth. The name that chimes a thousand notes of redemption for every woman who has ever been devastated by loss, struggled as a stranger, lived with the bitter, longed to be loved, fought for crumbs, or wept along the journey. She is an emblem of grace for every flawed and ailing sinner who has lived in her wake, not because of her own nobility but because of the One under whose wings she had come to trust—the God of Israel.

Because of Ruth's exquisite journey, her story becomes a remarkable setting for us to engage with God about our own stories. She is a flesh-and-blood example of integrity, kindness, purity, commitment, faith, and hard work. She is godliness with its sleeves rolled up, expressing her love for God even when she was profoundly devastated and left with a mother-in-law who had changed her name to "Bitter." (I think this means they weren't baking a lot of cookies together.) All this in the middle of a culture distinctly hostile to Israel's God.

Perhaps you can relate to Ruth's plight and her journey's challenges. You've struggled with the daunting dynamic of being a woman and a follower of Christ in an environment that doesn't always promote your beliefs or your gender. Or maybe you feel well supported but you've quietly wept in your singleness, longing for a man to choose you ... only you. Maybe you've been blessed with intimacy but you've been struggling to love that one person in your life you'd like to rename Bitter—or something else not as nice. Or maybe you've been completely shattered by a recent loss, or one far removed that has left a wound still bleeding. Or perhaps you've never done a Bible study before but the story of Ruth sounds intriguing and you're willing to give it a try.

No matter why you're here, I wholeheartedly welcome you to the *Living Room Series* where we will greet a woman from the pages of Scripture we will all be the better for knowing. And, of course, I invite you to do this in the context of a warm community where authenticity and vulnerability aren't so scary. That's why this book is filled with not only pages of Bible study but also recipes, original songs, a Web site *(www.livingroomseries.com),* and personal stories from Alli, Lauri, Carrie and Anadara—the four women who have studied, cooked, and eaten their way through this book (and *No Other Gods)* well before it ever made it to print. You will get to know their stories as we go, mostly finding that you are not alone, no matter where you are in your journey with God.

So grab your favorite recipes, closest friends, most exotic strangers (if you're up for it), darkest coffee, weightiest pen, and dearest Bible, and sink into your favorite living room.

Ruth and her God await you ...

Kelly

SESSION 01
TWO JOURNEYS

I CAN'T FORGET THE DAY I MET LORRAINE.

THE 60-YEAR-OLD, GRAY-HAIRED, LIGHT-HEARTED PILATES INSTRUCTOR WELCOMED A FRIEND AND ME INTO HER STUDIO WE NOW LOVINGLY DEEM, "LORRAINE'S HOUSE OF PAIN." WHO KNEW SUCH A KIND LADY COULD MAKE ME CRY SO MUCH? THAT HOLDING MY LEGS IN THE AIR, GRABBING THE BOTTOMS OF MY FEET, OR MAKING PERFECT CIRCLES WITH MY TOES COULD BE SUCH TORTURE? THE TIGHTLY WOUND WILL SUFFER UNDER SUCH SEEMINGLY INNOCENT EXERCISES, I'M JUST SAYING. AND DO NOT LET A SWEET LITTLE NAME LIKE *Lorraine* FOOL YOU—SHE'S STRONGER AND MORE NIMBLE THAN I'LL EVER BE, WHICH IS TERRIBLY DE-MOTIVATING WITH ALL MY "YOUTH" AND STUFF.

Despite the challenges, I was determined to master the exercises to make my bad back better. I was tired of being in pain, weary of not being able to do things I wanted to do like sit, run, hold children, or bend down to slide chocolate chip cookies out of the oven. Lorraine insisted I could get better if I agreed to one thing: strengthen my core. It sounded a little hocus-pocus, but I was desperate and apparently wanting for new forms of affliction.

A year later and Lorraine's House of Pain continues to be a place where I moan and whimper for an hour a session but, surprisingly enough, with almost no back pain. After several months and a lot of hard work, my core is strong. It is silly how enthused I am about the whole thing. My friends are sick of hearing me talk about it. They really don't want to see me touch my toes, again; they're not nearly as interested as you might think in my newly elongated spine.

But if you will allow me to tarry on the subject of *core* the spiritual parallels are inviting. Just as the cores of our physical bodies are engaged in everything we do, we must also give proper significance to our spiritual cores. I remember this truth taking shape for me when I noticed this striking concept, "For physical training is of some value, *but godliness has value for all things, holding promise for both the present life and the life to come*" (I Tim. 4:8, emphasis added).

I'd never realized that godliness held value for *all* things. I suppose I hadn't thought of it being this practical, this all-encompassing. For church and extra spiritual activities, yes, but for regular stuff, I wasn't so sure. In addition to such a sweeping statement, Paul (the writer of Timothy) said that godliness holds promise not only for eternal life but for our immediate, present, actual lives. This means it holds promise at our jobs, in our relationships, at the store, in our marriages, on vacation, and at the gym. Godliness affects things. It matters not just on the front row of church or when we get to heaven but in all things, right now.

Like anything, strengthening our spiritual cores requires training and a measure of dedication. It involves time and commitment and a little direction, which is where a Bible study can be really effective. But it mostly requires our hearts. Going through religious motions doesn't usually prove terribly rewarding in the spiritual realm. I only know this because I've spun a lot of energy on some pretty admirable activities that left me exhausted and frustrated when my heart wasn't engaged.

This heart-engagement is where Lorraine always gets me in Pilates. "Don't skimp on the old family recipe," she likes to say when I'm slacking in the middle of a routine exercise, half-heartedly plowing through the motions. I think the point is for us not to let familiarity with something make us think we don't have to give it our all. Seeking God with our whole hearts through the age-old avenues of Scripture, prayer, and fellowship will always prove valuable, no matter how many times we've heard it.

Because I know how easy it is for me to let the core spiritual disciplines slip (skimping on the family recipe), I really don't want you to skimp over the next six weeks when so much is at stake. The Book of Ruth is so infinitely remarkable that I want you to drink the last dregs of it, sipping on truths and principles that the Holy Spirit uniquely reveals to you—things I may never have conceived. So if you get interested in a cross reference, read the story around it; if a verse tugs at your heart, put everything down for a minute and refresh yourself from its well. You've got permission to dig, scrape, investigate, and go beyond the borders of these pages. And if all this sounds too daunting and over-achieverish, just stick to what's in front of you, but give it your all for the next six weeks—your core will be so happy!

DAY 01 TWO JOURNEYS
FLEEING HOME

When you grow up wearing proper Sunday School dresses and learning about Adam and Eve before you've heard of Bert and Ernie, it's sometimes hard to determine when that first introduction took place, how you felt, and what you thought. I could have been sucking on a pacifier the first time I heard Ruth's name. In most ways, I am really grateful that I got to hear both the great and not-so-great names of Scripture resounding off the walls before words had been formed on my tongue.

But if we're talking about cognizant memories, my first encounter with the Book of Ruth took place as I sat in the hunter green pews of Reston Bible Church—the church my dad founded a year before I was born and still pastors—listening to a borderline gruff, elderly Englishman named Major Ian Thomas. He spoke on the Book of Ruth for almost two hours, and if I recall correctly, I was spellbound. That's saying a lot for a 12-year-old who might prefer being somewhere else on a Friday night.

I remember Major Thomas not merely presenting the text but also exposing the fascinating symbolism that runs throughout the Book of Ruth like a camouflaged thread. He spoke as if he were tugging on some mysterious code, revealing the real story behind the story (revelations we will soon discover). For effect he really should have carried a magnifying glass and worn a fedora, but he was distinctly against hats in the sanctuary so this probably wouldn't have flown. This great man of the faith has since gone on to be with the Lord, but I am grateful to remember him as someone who kindled a love in my heart for the person of Ruth and, more importantly, her God—even Jesus hinted at in the pages of this Old Testament story.

Today I am anxious to begin surveying the context and setting of this amazingly small but powerful book with you. If you're like me, you'd just as soon skip the preliminary information and get right to the action, except it makes our understanding of Ruth's story so much richer when we understand the surroundings. It's sort of like pulling back the shades in your hotel room and remembering, "Oh yeah, I'm in Chicago!" To me, that always means three things: real coffee, tiramisu, and pizza. Context tells us a lot.

www.livingroomseries.com
Kelly and the girls talk about the food and the study—Why Ruth?

Carefully read Ruth 1:1-2. Elimelech's family lived in Bethlehem-Judah, and they were called _____.

To be an Ephrathite simply meant to be from Bethlehem-Judah, which was also known as Ephratah. It will be important for us to know throughout our study that Bethlehem was in ancient Israel, so that meant Elimelech's family were also considered Israelites. (Sort of like being a New Yorker also means you're an American.)

Why did Elimelech and Naomi leave Bethlehem-Judah for Moab? (Circle your answer below.)

There was a famine in Bethlehem.
There was a war in Bethlehem.
They had relatives in Moab.
A judge ordered them to leave.

Read Genesis 19:30-38. What do these verses say about the origin of the Moabites?

For more insight read Deuteronomy 23:3-6 and Judges 3:12-14. Describe from these verses the relationship between the Israel-ites and the Moabites.

Understanding the history of Moab and their relationship with Israel changes the tone of Elimelech and Naomi's journey. It's not like they were Americans heading to Canada. This was an enemy of Israel, a nation the Lord had historically commanded His children not to be in relationship with. Although he applauds Elimelech's zeal to take care of his family, Matthew Henry eloquently wrote, "I see not how his removal into the country of Moab, upon this occasion, could be justified ... the seed of Israel were now fixed, and ought not to remove into the territories of the heathen."[1]

After the Lord freed the Israelites from the land of Egypt, they wandered in the desert for 40 years. They lived as vagabonds, their tents pulled up and pinned down over and over like finicky campers. Then one day Joshua led them across the Jordan River into Canaan, the land of promise that flowed with milk and honey but, perhaps more importantly, with permanence. God had given them a home, and they didn't need to look elsewhere.

The city of Bethlehem, where Elimilech's family lived, was a hill country in the land of Judah and part of the promised land of Canaan. Interestingly enough, *Bethlehem* means "House of Bread," and there hadn't been much of that since their departure. So perhaps you're thinking, *If God had given the Israelites a permanent place to live where He promised to take care of them, why the famine?*

> **Read Judges 2:11-19. Do you see any evidence for why there was a famine in the land? If so, explain your answer.**

> **For Discussion: When Alli, Lauri, Carrie, Anadara, and I studied this Scripture, one question that came up was, *Does God still work like this today?* Use Scripture to support your thoughts.**

> **What tended to happen to the people when a judge died (v. 19)?**

> **Now look back at Ruth 1:1 (NIV) and fill in the blank: "In the days when the _____ ruled, there was a famine in the land."**

It's important to note that the story of Ruth took place during the time of the Judges, a period of approximately 450 years when God raised up judges to rule over Israel. Clearly these verses in the Book of Judges show us the people had a history of turning to God during seasons of punishment but forgetting Him during seasons of prosperity.

> **Personal Take: Are you currently in a season of trial, blessing, or both? Describe how your current circumstances negatively or positively affect your relationship with God.**

The people had a history of turning to God during seasons of punishment but forgetting Him during seasons of prosperity.

I'm so happy to write that I'm in a great season at the moment. My family is strong, my relationships sweet, and I'm in a new house with a walnut tree in the yard that intermittently drops hard green walnut balls onto my roof that sound like miniature bombs while I write. It is a wonderful time. Although I will be honest in saying that it's in seasons like these when I have to be more purposeful about my pursuit of the Lord in Scripture, study, and prayer. These don't come quite as naturally when life is smooth and the walnut trees are bombing.

I want to close the day by drawing Elimelech and Naomi's plight back to our own. Here they stood on the precipice of a sticky decision—to stay in the arid land of God's choosing or to flee to the bountiful one God had roped off. We know that Elimelech chose the latter, but the question today is *What will you choose?* Perhaps the Lord has you in difficult circumstances and the attractive land of Moab is an alluring decision away. Escaping to easier terrain is all too tempting when we're weary in hardship.

> Escaping to easier terrain is all too tempting when we're weary in hardship.

Ponder Galatians 6:9 and Hebrews 11:24-26, and then write about how these verses encourage you to stand firm where God has you. Be as thoughtful and detailed as you can.

Be encouraged by this quote from Matthew Henry, reminding us that fleeing our circumstances doesn't necessarily remedy them. "It is our wisdom to make the best of that which is, for it is seldom that changing our place is mending it."[2]

God is present right where you are. Stay put and stand firm. It is always more blessed to be under the care of His will than anywhere else—no matter how green the grass or bountiful the walnut trees.

DAY 02 TWO JOURNEYS
RETURNING HOME

The first chapter of Ruth is a story of two journeys: The journey from Bethlehem to Moab and the journey from Moab back to Bethlehem. The first is briefly described in the two verses we studied yesterday, but the second journey, the journey of return, takes the rest of the chapter.

> **Before looking at today's reading, reread Ruth 1:1-2 . Who were the four people who traveled from Bethlehem to Moab?**

> **Just to refresh your memory, all four family members were from Bethlehem and were called what? (Circle your answer below.)**

> **Bethlehemites   Canaanites   Ephrathites   Amorites**

> **They were from the town of Bethlehem and the nation of _____. (See the top of p. 12 if you need help.)**

> **Now that we've got some of the technical details down, read verses 3-7 through a couple of times. Take a moment to appreciate the gravity of such tragic circumstances.**

One of the most significant differences between the journey from Bethlehem to Moab and the journey from Moab back to Bethlehem is the difference in people. Naomi was the only one to take both journeys. Though she left with two sons and a husband, she was returning with two women who were not her flesh and blood.

> **Write the names of the daughters-in-law below, their nationality, and the sons of Naomi's that each of them had married. (See 4:10 to deduce who Ruth and Orpah were married to.)**

> _____ _____ _____
>   name   nationality   married to

> _____ _____ _____
>   name   nationality   married to

According to I Kings 11:1-4, why might it have been a problem for Mahlon and Kilion to marry Moabite women?

In Deuteronomy 7 the Lord commanded the people of Israel not to intermarry with certain nations. First Kings 11 shows us a specific example why entering into a covenant relationship with these nations presented a significant problem. Solomon's heart was led astray to other gods because of his marriages to women from other nations who didn't regard the one true God. Ultimately, his heart was not fully devoted to the Lord.

We are to love and reach out to all people.

Note that God's commandments were not against the races of these people, but instead, their rejection of Him. It is the same concept found in 2 Corinthians 6:14, where the apostle Paul instructed us not to be unequally yoked with unbelievers. We are to love and reach out to all people, but we are not to compromise our love for the Lord by attaching ourselves by covenant to those who don't share this same love. This principle in Ruth, Deuteronomy, and 1 Kings will be of even greater significance to us in coming days, so hang on to it.

Why did Naomi decide to return to Bethlehem (Ruth 1:6-7)?

Personal Response: Have you ever turned back to God out of desperation or necessity? If so, describe it here.

Read Luke 15:11-20 and list as many similarities as you can find between Naomi's situation and the son in this account.

I can't help but note that the driving force behind Naomi's choices to leave Bethlehem, and later Moab, was the same—a desire for physical nourishment. It would be especially hard for me, of all people, to fault anyone for being motivated by such a thing as food. If Moab had been known for its fresh mozzarella and olive oil, I might have moved too. But sarcasm aside, the catalyst behind both journeys seems to be governed by the physical and not the spiritual. On both occasions their physical circumstances and not necessarily the God of their circumstances dictated their decisions.

I deeply admire some of my friends for heeding the Lord over their natural desires. Three in particular have chosen to stay in tough marriages when divorce continually cries as the easier option. I went to elementary school with a friend who unexpectedly got pregnant in college and, while abortion may have seemed the obvious answer, she committed to having the baby who is now a beautiful, blonde teenager. God's ways are not always the most practical, popular, or unopposed, but they are the most blessed. I wonder how Elimelech and Naomi's lives would have been different had they been directed by the supernatural over the natural and stayed in the land of Judah.

> **God's ways are not always the most practical, popular, or unopposed, but they are the most blessed.**

Personal Response: Have you ever allowed your circumstances to direct you instead of leaving room for God's direction? In what specific ways can you act on God's leading?

For Discussion: I can understand why Naomi decided to return to her homeland when she found out the famine had passed, but why do you think Ruth and Orpah decided to go with her? (Remember, Naomi's family moved to a foreign country out of need, but what might Ruth's and Orpah's reasons have been?)

While Naomi was in the land of Moab she heard that the Lord had come to the aid of His people (v. 6). The great pastor and scholar, Warren Wiersbe, made this moving statement, "How sad it is when people only *hear* about God's blessing, but never experience it, because they are not in the place where God can bless them."[3]

I can identify with Naomi when I hear from the distant land of my own choosing about the warm glow of God's provision and presence for someone or somewhere else. I have pouted against Him in my disobedience, angry that I wasn't experiencing Him but not wanting to change my allegiances either. In these times I often experience God's gracious pursuit of me even when my heart is cold and far away. Notice that Naomi's return to Bethlehem wasn't necessarily out of a longing for her God but for His provision. Yet God used this basic desire for food to pull her back to Himself, wanting to bless her immeasurably.

Personal Response: Think of a time when God pursued you—even drew you—when you were in a far-off place. Jot down just enough detail to remind you of the story for sharing with the individuals in your group.

When Naomi heard that God had come to help her people in Bethlehem, she and her daughters-in-law prepared to return home (v. 6). My friend April noted the word *prepared* and gave me a mini-sermon over lunch about how it takes preparation to return home. She thought of all the things that would have encompassed for Naomi, Ruth, and Orpah; and she likened it to her own spiritual journey, remembering the things that turning back to God required of her. She left me with Psalm 16 as a benediction—a fitting tie-in about the place God intends for us to dwell.

In closing meditate on Psalm 16:1-6. If you need to return to God in some way, write about the preparations you're willing to make. If you are where you need to be, write about the details of verses 5-6.

No matter where you find yourself today—flourishing in His presence or struggling on your own terms—bread is always available at His table for anyone willing to return.

DAY 03 TWO JOURNEYS
WEEPING FORWARD

For the past few months I taught a Wednesday night Bible study for some fabulous women from The Next Door ministry in downtown Nashville. This ministry assists its residents who have recently been released from prison and helps them successfully transition back into free society. Each woman agrees to live on its premises for six months, participate in counseling, attend a weekly Bible study, work a solid job, address her addictions, and assume other responsibilities. As you can imagine, it's a spicy group where raw is in and sugarcoated is most definitely out. They need all their energy for survival, so there's not a lot left over for religious affectation. Their honesty and vulnerability is what I love so much about these women, mostly because when God hits their lives, it's the real deal. You can't fake transformation in shoes like theirs.

These girls are some of the most courageous women I know, forging ahead on a journey that will take them back to the place from which they came—the outside world. Many seek to return to family, distant homes, past careers, and dear friends. They hope for fresh starts and new lives, all of them convinced that success is only possible if they return changed. Going back the same person is not an option.

Naomi's journey is strikingly similar. Today we find her packing her bags and hitting the road back to Judah. We find her returning to the place she left. She's hardly the same person, but in this case the change is not necessarily for the better. She is heading back without her husband or sons, bitter at God, and with two trailing daughters-in-law she wishes would just leave her alone already because she's not in the in-law, let's-have-tea mood right now. This is not the way I want my Next Door girls to return to their homes, but then again, Naomi probably never imagined it this way either, and who can blame her despairing posture? How gracious that God was already in Bethlehem waiting for her, waiting for whoever else would choose to come with her, stranger or not. Naomi just didn't know it yet. We'll see in the weeks to come that God's grace is always positioned for anyone who will simply come, often for the ones who don't even know it.

> God's grace is always positioned for anyone who will simply come.

Today's reading is Ruth 1:7-14. Slowly take in all the details.

Naomi said, "May the LORD show kindness to you, as you have shown to your dead and to me" (v. 8). The word "kindness" is an unfortunately weak translation of the Hebrew word *hesed,* a huge word throughout the book. It is described this way by a few different authors:

> A strong relational term that wraps up in itself an entire cluster of concepts, all the positive attributes of God—love, mercy, grace, kindness, goodness, benevolence, loyalty, covenant faithfulness: in short, that quality that moves a person to act for the benefit of another without respect to the advantage it might bring to the one who expresses it. [4]

> Israel associated it *[hesed]* with Yahweh's covenant relationship with her … despite her waywardness, Yahweh always stood steadfastly by Israel in "covenant loyalty."[5]

> Love, grace, mercy, kindness—all of the positive acts of devotion that flow out of a covenantal relationship.[6]

I want to emphasize the word *hesed* because it represents a significant theme throughout the book and will be used several times.

Briefly describe *hesed* in the margin using your own words.

Given that the word was often used as a unique, covenant-love between God and Israel, how is it significant that Naomi asked God to show *hesed* to Ruth and Orpah?

For Discussion: Has someone shown you *hesed?* If so, describe the person and what this extraordinary love means to you.

Even though I've read this story many times, for some reason I always thought Naomi urged Ruth and Orpah to stay in Moab *before* they set out on their trip.

Where did Naomi's discussion with her daughters-in-law actually take place (v. 7)?

Note that Naomi, Ruth, and Orpah had packed their bags, left their homes, and had gotten down the road when Naomi started urging them to go back. It's sort of like being a kid on vacation, stuffed in the family station wagon, six hours from home when you start fighting with your siblings and your dad promises he's not afraid to turn this car right around if everyone doesn't shape up. The terrible thought of turning around after getting so far down the road usually prompted a temporary truce for the Minter kids—at least for five more minutes.

What reason did Naomi first give them for returning to Moab?

In verse 10, who turned back? (Circle your answer below.)

Ruth   Orpah   both Ruth and Orpah   neither

Naomi realized she had two very determined and committed in-laws on her hands. When they didn't take her hint, she kicked up her argument a notch as if to say, "The only reason you're following me to Bethlehem is because I'm your only hope for another husband. Even if I got married and pregnant with another son tonight, you'd have to wait 20 years for him to grow up, and that might be a little sketchy anyhow. So your best bet is just to cut me and your losses and find another husband your own age in Moab who can take care of you. Oh, and also, the Lord's hand has totally gone out against me—just in case the other stuff I mentioned wasn't convincing enough."

After Naomi's compelling argument, verse 14 says, "At this they _____ again."

One of my closest friends moved from Boone, North Carolina, to Nashville three years ago. She had lived in Boone for 20 years and had made a home whose roots held almost as firm as the surrounding Appalachian Mountains. Leaving was not really an option until the Lord opened up a very specific job for her in Nashville and the Holy Spirit's leading became even stronger than those mountains she awoke to every morning. Through months of tears and grief, she packed her bags, made the journey, and dug a new foundation in Tennessee. Fortunately for me, she landed about a mile down the road. My friend wept, but she wept forward.

My friend wept, but she wept forward.

Although there will be
weeping in this life, the
direction in which we weep
is what truly matters.

Verse 14 is one of the most meaningful verses to me in all of Scripture because it poignantly reminds me that although there will be weeping in this life, the direction in which we weep is what truly matters.

> According to Ruth 1:7-14, who wept going forward and who wept going backward? Describe your answer below.

> Personal Take: The verses say Orpah kissed her mother-in-law good-bye, but Ruth clung to her. What do you think motivated their decisions? There's not necessarily a "right" answer, but given what you know so far, be as thoughtful as you can.

> This idea of weeping in different directions is very relevant to us. In the following passages compare and contrast both characters. Specifically, how did their grief affect their direction?

> Apostle Paul   Rich Young Man
> Acts 20:22,36-38   Mark 10:17-22

The apostle Paul wept but didn't allow his grief to stop his forward motion while the rich young man walked away from Christ with great sadness. It's difficult to point a finger at Orpah or the rich young ruler because we too may have turned back in the face of loss or adversity. But how great the honor and reward of Ruth and Paul who, in their tears, kept walking forward.

> Personal Response: Are you in a season of grief that makes you want to stop or turn around? Have you ever experienced moving forward with the Lord even in the midst of weeping? Write about your experience below.

Be encouraged. God sees your tears. Cry them, wipe them, feel them, but don't let them stop you. It's possible to cry *and* walk.

DAY 04 TWO JOURNEYS
A LONG OBEDIENCE

Does it feel like we're creeping through the Book of Ruth? I realize we're only to verse 14 and it's taken us three days to get here, but for whatever it's worth, I'm really enjoying the slow pace as we wade the depths of such a rich book. Any faster and we might miss the buried diamonds and concealed treasures. I'd like to think we're smelling the roses as we go, sort of like my niece, Maryn, who's just learning to walk and pauses with every step to pick up the exciting pebble or tattered leaf. Of course she can only pick up one new item at a time because she carries her toothbrush with her wherever she goes—she's into hygiene. If she could speak beyond her excessive vocabulary of "No" and "Mama" (short for her dog, Murphy, *not* her mother who birthed her), she might be saying, *Why rush through life when you've got this amazing toothbrush to examine?* It will help us to harness this attitude.

Read Ruth 1:15. (See what I mean?)

It's interesting that even after Orpah went home, Naomi refused to abandon her In-laws-Turn-Back campaign. She wasn't going down easily.

How many times did Naomi urge Ruth to turn back (vv. 8-15)?

Name two reasons why Naomi encouraged Ruth to go back (v. 15).

Personal Take: Why do you think Naomi was so adamant about not having Ruth and Orpah return to Bethlehem with her?

Although the text really doesn't tell us, Warren Wiersbe suggests that it's possible Naomi was trying to cover the fact that her sons had married Moabites (outside the covenant nation of Israel). If she returned home alone, perhaps no one would ever know.[7]

Whatever the reason might have been, we just can't miss how many times Ruth had to deflect Naomi's discouraging persuasions to turn back. This is an important principle, as obedience to God is often wrought with a slew of obstacles that persuade us to change our minds. I used to think that my choice to obey in any given situation was a one-time decision, but I now realize that obedience might mean having to make that same choice several times in a week, month, or year. We saw in yesterday's reading that Orpah successfully dodged Naomi's first deluge of discouragement (v. 10), but after Naomi's second and third push, she gave in.

Personal Response: Describe a time when you committed to obedience but experienced defeat after one or two obstacles. OR, describe a time when, by God's grace, you held firm even in the midst of several trials or temptations to respond otherwise. What do you think preserved your obedience?

I find the idea of sustained obedience difficult in a myriad of situations but distinctly so when it comes to any kind of addiction. Just yesterday I had coffee with one of my amazingly talented musician friends who is a recovering alcoholic. To quote Friedrich Nietzsche (of all people), my friend's commitment to stay dry is "A long obedience in the same direction."[8] There is rarely a day in his industry when the temptation is not present in some form. And yet for over two years he has relied on the strength and grace of God to refuse every alluring drop, a sustained obedience I'm convinced rises to the heavens as a fragrant aroma to our Savior.

Often times I can closely relate to Orpah, who made the right decision once but couldn't hang on after further persuasions. But now I am learning the art of prolonged obedience as modeled so gracefully by Ruth and my musician friend. This principle makes me think of Joseph and a period when his master's wife persistently tried to seduce him.

Read Genesis 39:6b-10 and fill in the blank from verse 10:

"Though she spoke to Joseph _____ _____ _____, he refused to go to bed with her or *even be with her.* "

I wonder how many times Joseph had to choose obedience in the face of temptation. He wouldn't have escaped her seductive trap had he only stood firm once. Instead, he was faced with making the same decision for righteousness day after day, much like Ruth stood firm in the face of Naomi's multiple persuasions. But I would hate for us to walk away from today's reading thinking that all we need is a little more willpower. I don't think Ruth's and Joseph's determined obedience had much to do with willpower at all, and to think so only encourages us to live by our own strength and self-righteousness. Instead, we see their motivation anchored in something far greater than their inner resolve.

> **You'll have to glance at tomorrow's reading to answer this, but compare Joseph's statement to his master's wife (Gen. 39:9) with Ruth's statement to Naomi (Ruth 1:16-17). Whom did Joseph and Ruth both reference?**

> **In what way did God factor into their obedience?**

We simply cannot miss that Ruth's and Joseph's commitment to obedience stemmed from their commitments to God. This is an enormous truth that will sustain us through times of temptation and trial that urge us to forsake the path we're on. We won't be able to last if our motivation is based on anything but our relationship with God. We may be able to resist once or twice like Orpah, but only a love for Christ will sustain a long-term commitment to obedience.

Only a love for Christ will sustain a long-term commitment to obedience.

> **Personal Response: Because enduring obedience hinges on our love for Jesus, can you pinpoint any weakness in your trust, love, or belief in Him that is affecting your resolve to obey?**

Look back at today's fill-in-the-blank verse from Genesis and notice the italicized words. Not only did Joseph refuse to go to bed with her, but he also refused to *even be with her*. Joseph changed his circumstances so he wouldn't be tempted to sin against the God he loved so deeply. It's easy to kid ourselves and justify our behavior when our hearts aren't really committed to God. But when we grasp His love and the truth that obedience is for our freedom, we will change our circumstances to protect our environment to obey. Perhaps no one changed her circumstances more than Ruth when she decided to leave her people, false gods, and homeland for the God of Israel.

Personal Response: Do you need to make a life change for the preservation of obedience? It can be large or small. Write about it here.

Ruth and Joseph each showed enormous resolve as they walked out their obedience to God while doing whatever it took to preserve such obedience. The Book of James touches on this beautifully.

Close by meditating on these fitting verses as you seek to live out a long obedience: James 1:2-4,12.

"Consider it a great joy, my brothers, whenever you experience various trials, knowing that the testing of your faith produces endurance. But endurance must do its complete work, so that you may be mature and complete, lacking nothing. ... Blessed is a man who endures trials, because when he passes the test he will receive the crown of life that He has promised to those who love Him" (HCSB).

DAY 05 TWO JOURNEYS
WHEREVER YOU GO

I burned my scrambled eggs this morning. I've been picking up farm fresh brown eggs from a local farm for the past four months, and I've gone a little crazy with my egg intake. Who knows what this has done to my cholesterol level, but doggone it if the stuff that's clogging my arteries isn't the healthiest, most organic sludge available. Nonetheless, the smell is really bad, and my dear friend with whom I share my home was not so pleased when she walked in to discover I had accidentally left the eggs on the stove until they were burned beyond recognition. She had the instinctive but not so helpful urge to vigorously light candles in every room so our house could smell like rotten eggs with a hint of honey-ginger or red currant, depending on which room we were in. I am now desperately trying to open every window, but we just moved into this 1930s house and most of the windows are painted shut. I'm thinking this is a fire hazard, but more seriously, it puts us at risk for trapped burned-egg smell.

I mention this because it's all I can think about because it's all I can smell. It also has just a little—and I do mean little—to do with our reading today as we visit one of the most celebrated passages in Scripture. We will see the importance of spouses, roommates, friends, relatives, children, and coworkers sticking together in times of adversity—like when the eggs are burned and you can't open the windows ... or something like that.

> **I know you glanced at these two verses yesterday, but read Ruth 1:16-17, taking special note because this is the first time we really hear from Ruth.**

> **Personal Take: Up to this point, Naomi had done all the talking, but then Ruth spoke up. Out of all the things she listed, write the words that resonate with you the most and explain why.**

I love that in essence Ruth respectfully, but strongly, said, "Enough already!" She wiped her tears and got a little aggressive, kindly putting an end to Naomi's dissenting remarks. She had finally had enough, and sometimes this isn't a bad place to be because it forces us to deal with the issue at hand.

In Ruth's case, how did her loving, yet firm, words to Naomi change her situation (v. 18)? (Underline your answer below.)

Naomi …

got mad and ran ahead	**disowned Ruth**
stopped trying to persuade Ruth	**hysterically cried**

Ruth's eloquent speech to Naomi uncovers an incredible treasure in our reading: the power of the spoken word. Many times I've gotten so discouraged by Satan, my own weak flesh, or another opposing entity, that I've finally resorted to speaking out loud the truth of Scripture. Audibly praying and reading Scripture is a wonderful discipline to employ, especially when you are overwhelmed. But keeping Ruth's words to Naomi in mind, today we'll look specifically at the use of our spoken words—especially as they relate to the people in our lives.

Briefly sum up the central thought of each of these verses:

Proverbs 16:23-24 _____

Proverbs 18:13 _____

Proverbs 25:11 _____

Proverbs 27:5-6 _____

Your Take: How do these principles from Proverbs play out in Ruth's conversation with Naomi?

Just last night I asked a friend over to discuss some misunderstandings. I had discovered that I had offended her, and I wanted to make things right. In case you're wondering if I enjoy these kinds of conversations, think about being shoved off a high dive and you'll be right at my level of awkwardness. The good news is that we both spoke honestly to one another, cleared some things up, and left with a sense of relief. I realize this isn't the direction these discussions always go, but even despite the hard things we had to address, the conversation was healing.

Because I grew up in a home where we were taught to talk things out respectfully, I am amazed at how many people don't know how to have difficult conversations. I say this with not a hint of judgment, as I would have no idea either had my parents not taught us at an early age how to deal with conflict. Still, I'm surprised at how many people I've seen refuse to have hard conversations. Instead, they harbor anger and unforgiveness, never allowing for an honest exchange. Lack of honest communication has to be one of the ultimate destroyers of relationships, while learning the quality of gracious but bold speech can be a balm in bitter and complicated situations.

> Learning the quality of gracious but bold speech can be a balm in bitter and complicated situations.

Without getting overly clinical with Ruth's eloquent speech, I want us to dissect some of the elements in the following passage:

> **Circle the words that show Ruth's determination and strength.**
> **Underline the words that show her love and support for Naomi.**
> **Check the words that show her spiritual conviction.**
> **Star the words that show her humility.**
> **(Mark words as many times as you think they apply.)**

> **"Don't urge me to leave you or to turn back from you. Where you go I will go, and where you stay I will stay. Your people will be my people and your God my God. Where you die I will die and there I will be buried. May the LORD deal with me, be it ever so severely, if anything but death separates you and me" (1:16-17).**

> **Now read verse 18 and take in Naomi's response to Ruth's words.**

The NIV starts out with "When Naomi realized." It took Ruth's strong resolve mingled with humble love to finally convince Naomi that Ruth wasn't taking *no* for an answer. It took Ruth's words to make her realize this. Why? Because, governed by the Holy Spirit, our words have great strength. Sometimes we need to speak the hard word. Sometimes we need to speak the word of forgiveness or the word of accepting forgiveness. Other times we need to speak the loving, determined, or committed word. Always the humble word.

Matthew 5:23-24
Therefore, if you are offering your gift at the altar and there remember that your brother has something against you, leave your gift there in front of the altar. First go and be reconciled to your brother; then come and offer your gift.

Personal Response: I know we're wading into sensitive waters, but do you need to speak a word to someone? Matthew 5:23-24 talks about the importance of not delaying in certain circumstances. If you are sensing the Holy Spirit's nudge, write it here.

The verses we've studied today have been read at a million weddings and printed on as many cards, gracing relationships since the day Ruth spoke them. We memorialize her words in the context of loving friendships and brides and grooms who are so zealously in love that the rest of us have to go drown ourselves in cake. But the truth is that this famous speech was uttered amidst loss and hardship and in the face of much bitterness. Ruth's words did not usher in a honeymoon for her but rather a permanent home in a foreign land. As we close week 1 of studying this phenomenal book, the obvious questions become: *Are we so committed to Christ? Will we go where He goes? Stay where He stays? Will His people be our people? His Father our Father?* I'm really looking forward to answering these questions with you over the next five weeks. You have done a remarkable job.

WHEREVER YOU GO

Connie Harrington & Kelly Minter
See the story behind the song at www.livingroomseries.com.

When your cup's full, when your road is open
Or when you've lost your light
I'll cling to you when you're whole or broken
Cause we're all broken sometimes

Chorus
Wherever you go I'll go
Wherever you stay I'll stay
The steepest of the steps you take we'll take together
I'm never gonna turn around
My place is where you are found
The promise I give you now will be forever

Lend me your tears, the ones you cry the hardest
We'll water the seeds you sow
One day you'll wake up and joy will be your harvest
And peace will be your home

Chorus

Bridge
Your people will be my people
Your God will be my God
Where your feet go I will follow
You're where I belong

Chorus

Kelly Minter & Connie Harrington. Warner-Tamerlane Publishing Corp. (BMI),
All For This Music (BMI), Made For This Music (BMI) Admin. by Warner-Tamerlane
Publishing Corp. (BMI) Mintyfresh Music (ASCAP)

CHICKEN ENCHILADAS
PRE-HEAT OVEN TO 350° SERVES 6-8

This is perhaps one of my all-time favorite dishes. It takes a little effort, but your group will love you for taking the time to tackle this one. (And it's even better the next day.)

6 chicken breasts (boiled 20 minutes; keep 2 cups broth)
2 cups canned chicken broth
8 burrito size tortillas
8 tablespoons picante sauce
½ cup tightly packed cilantro
½ cup sour cream
1 teaspoon cumin (I use more)
1 tablespoon flour
½ stick of butter
4 oz. grated jack cheese
4 oz. grated cheddar cheese
1 can black beans, optional

Directions:
In blender combine cumin, cilantro, sour cream, 1 cup canned chicken broth, and 1 cup reserved chicken broth. In skillet or saucepan, heat butter slowly and add flour until smooth. Slowly add 2 remaining cups of chicken broth until smooth and creamy (I usually add more flour to make it thicker). Add to sauce in blender. This is the "gravy."

To make enchiladas: Take each tortilla and fill with ⅓ cup shredded chicken and 1-2 tablespoons of picante sauce. Add black beans if desired. Roll tortillas and place in 9x13" pan, seam side down. Fill pan with gravy, completely covering the enchiladas. Sprinkle cheeses on top. Bake at 350° uncovered for 30 minutes.

MEXICAN ICE CREAM SUNDAE
SERVES 6

Lauri pulled this out during one of our last gatherings. We were putting the cinnamon whipped cream on anything we could find. It's a Lauri original, easy and sophisticated.

1 quart of good vanilla ice cream
1 cup sliced almonds
¼ cup sugar

Put almonds in small saucepan with ¼ cup sugar. Cook over low heat, stirring constantly until sugar has melted and coated the almonds. This will take a while, but don't try to speed it up! When all are coated, dump onto plate and allow to cool. These should break up pretty easily. Set aside.

CINNAMON WHIPPED CREAM

2 cups heavy whipping cream
¼ cup sugar
½ teaspoon cinnamon

In the mixer bowl of an electric mixer put the heavy whipping cream, ¼ cup sugar, and ½ teaspoon cinnamon. With the whisk attachment, blend at low speed until consistency is thick enough to turn it up. Turn to med-high speed until stiff peaks form on the end of the whisk. Test it to get the texture that you want. Just don't overbeat it. Set aside.

Assemble: Scoop some ice cream into a dish, add a scoop of whipped cream and sprinkle with almonds and extra cinnamon if you want! The best part is the leftover almonds to munch on and whipped cream to add to your coffee.

ARRIVING

ARRIVING. IT TENDS TO DENOTE THE GLEE OF MUCH-ANTICIPATED DESTINATIONS AND THE END OF LONG JOURNEYS.

DURING OUR SUMMER VACATIONS WHEN I WAS LITTLE, MY MOM AND DAD WOULD WAKE THE FOUR OF US KIDS AROUND TWO IN THE MORNING, CARRY US OUTSIDE, AND SLING US INTO THE BACK OF OUR SLENDER LIGHT BLUE STATION WAGON, HOPING TO GET IN A FEW MINUTES OF QUIET DRIVING WHILE WE SLUMBERED IN OUR SLEEPING BAGS. THIS WAS, OF COURSE, BEFORE IPODS AND IN-CAR TELEVISIONS, SO IT WAS UP TO TRAVEL-YAHTZEE™ AND CONNECT FOUR™ TO OCCUPY OUR ATTENTION BEFORE "WHEN ARE WE GONNA GET THERE?" STARTED SOUNDING FROM THE BACKSEAT LIKE A TRAIN ON MY DAD'S HEELS.

Though most remember their family vacations as similarly chaotic, I promise that Minter vacations remain in a class all their own. Most of this had to do with being on a pastor's budget, which I don't regret for a moment because had we been on any other budget my dad would have been something other than a pastor, and this has been one of my greatest joys. This being so, we stayed at a lot of free and cheap places that color my childhood memories. Places that people from the church would either give us or recommend. The problem was not so much where we ended up but the vehicles we took to get there.

Whether it was the station wagon, the four-cylinder, stick-shift mini-van, or my grandparents' sedan we borrowed just so we wouldn't break down, we broke down. Every time. Especially the mini-van. It just couldn't handle the six of us plus the car-top carrier, not to mention it had a car malady called vapor lock that flared up on long trips. I know you've never heard of vapor lock before because you grew up in a normal family that went on normal vacations and took normal cars to get there, or you were a billionaire and you flew. We broke down so many times that my brother, David, grew up believing cars weren't designed to travel those kinds of distances. Like using a bicycle to get across the Atlantic, they just weren't made for that kind of thing.

REMARKS
MELROSE - 1ST STOP
CONNECTION TO WASSAIC
FORDHAM - 1ST STOP
FORDHAM - 1ST STOP
WHITE PLAINS - 1ST STOP
TIME TRK DESTINATION REMARKS
2:59 105 NO. WH PLAINS FORDHAM - 1ST STOP
3:17 30 SOUTHEAST WHITE PLAINS - 1ST STOP
3:20 109 NO. WH PLAINS MT. VERNON WEST - 1ST STOP
3:23 107 NO. WH PLAINS MELROSE - 1ST STOP
3:46 15 WASSAIC WHITE PLAINS - 1ST STOP
METRO-NORTH TICKETS

One of our favorite vacation spots was in New Hampshire overlooking Lake Sunapee. It came with sailboats, a dingy, kayaks, and a red and white Donzi that belonged to the neighbor. He'd pull us around on tubes, kneeboards, and skis in water that never got above "icy," even in July, but when you're a kid you can't be bothered with such trifling things.

Raspberries lined the lake, extraordinary trails snaked up verdant hills, and fishing occupied me for hours from the sloping wood dock that jetted out over the brilliant green water. When I got up early enough, I'd cast alongside real fishermen, natives of the north and sea. One time one looked at me and asked—"Fishin-foh-dinnah?"—as though it were one word. To which I asked him six times to repeat himself, eventually responding with a polite smile, and a "No, I'm 12 and my mom's making spaghetti tonight." I loved catching fish but never was much for finagling them off the hook, much less filleting them for "dinnah."

Then there was the cabin in Canada, owned by a wonderful but far more adventurous family in our church than the Minter clan could ever hope to be. Before we left, they stoked our anticipation with stories of piles of fresh blueberries and the lake with its turquoise hue; but they forgot to mention the outhouse and the hatchet for chopping wood. It was a really amazing place for people who didn't mind roughing it; my dad could have stayed there a month. My mom, however, doesn't do hatchets. And she contended you needed a machete just to get to the outhouse, assuming you were willing to go there in the first place.

The significantly bigger problem was the "mouse" that scurried across the floor, (my little sister Katie's rendering). My mom quickly clarified: it wasn't a mouse, and it didn't run. It was a rat that sauntered across the kitchen like it was the landlord. This particular rodent became the deal breaker for everyone but Dad, though even he knew he couldn't expect his family to bunk with animals and borrow hatchets, no matter how great the crackling fires or fresh the blueberries. We found another cabin the next morning on Spectacle Lake with an indoor bathroom. Arriving never felt better.

If long and highly anticipated journeys make for extra spectacular arrivals, this week's study will not disappoint. As we witness Naomi pass through the city gates she hadn't seen in over 12 years, we will watch her greet old friends and acquaintances, though, tragically, without her husband and children. For Naomi, her arrival will mark a significant return to her homeland. For Ruth, Bethlehem will prove a foreign land, rife with challenges for a widowed Moabitess. But both will arrive—and in a story that's already been marked with bitter loss, weeping, and the tearing apart of two sisters, just this stands for an awful lot.

DAY 01 ARRIVING
COMING HOME

I have a friend, Holly, who's 48 and has six children, the oldest being six, and another friend, Mary Katharine, who took the oldest four to her house yesterday—this is starting to sound like one of those dreaded story problems—for a viewing of the scariest movie, hands down, ever made: *The Wizard Of Oz.* I told her I thought this was a huge mistake; that I didn't think kids under five should be subjected to this movie because I was 20 the last time it scared me. I don't care what anyone says, nothing is more frightening than that green witch on her bicycle pedaling through the air referring to Dorothy as "my pretty."

Second to the witch are possibly those monkeys. Then add the diminishing hourglass, a Wizard who's the only one who can help but who ends up not really being a Wizard, stranding Dorothy in Oz with a cowardly lion, a scarecrow without a brain or a heart or an eye or something, and a tin-can man who has to oil himself to walk. But none of this even touches the worst of it! The true horror of this film lies in the simplest but most terrifying of scenarios: Dorothy can't get home.

Hence, the movie that made world-famous the tapping together of two ruby red shoes and the reciting of one of the most memorable phrases of our day, "There's no place like home. There's no place like home. There's no place like home."

I'm assuming Naomi carried the same sentiment, sans her ruby reds, on the long hike back to Bethlehem. Truly life had taken multiple tragic turns since her departure, making her return either especially sweet or deeply bitter. We will soon find out. Either way, I wonder whether every worn step hit the dust with the ebbing hope that things might be different in Bethlehem—different because when one is in the land of Oz, Moab, or any unfamiliar place, there truly is no place like home.

Carefully read Ruth 1:19-21 two times through.

On Naomi's return "the whole town was stirred" (v. 19). The key Hebrew word here is *wattehom* meaning "echoed with excitement." The word "conjures up images of joyous shouting and happy, animated conversations in response to an event. … Here one imagines excited citizens scurrying about the streets shouting the good news to others, who then do likewise."[1]

Personal Take: Does the town's excited reaction surprise you or would you have expected it? What does this reaction say about Naomi and her history with the people of Bethlehem? Explain your thoughts below.

www.livingroomseries.com Get a glimple of Kelly and the "nogs" as they get together to study the Book of Ruth.

It's interesting that verse 19 says the town was stirred because of "them." This relays that not only Naomi's arrival caused a reaction.

Given what we know about the Moabites' relationship with Israel, describe the significance of Naomi returning to Bethlehem with Ruth.

This stirring reception seems to indicate Naomi was not an obscure individual in Bethlehem but had been a well-loved, prominent person in her society. So much so that her return set the entire town in a frenzy, the women exclaiming to one another, "Can this be Naomi?" Interestingly, this celebrated recognition didn't soothe Naomi's pain but seemed to exacerbate it. Naomi now stood empty handed, a poignant contrast to the fullness by which she had once been known: married to a prominent man in Bethlehem, the mother of two sons, bearing the name *Naomi,* which literally means "lovely," and being part of the chosen nation of Israel. In her time and culture these collective attributes deemed her rich beyond measure. Contrast this picture with the woman now standing at the gates of the city bereft of everything she held dear except a foreign woman from a despised land.

Timothy Keller can help us further understand the cultural ramifications of Naomi's desperate situation:

"It is difficult for us today to appreciate the significance of child-bearing in ancient times. We live in an individualistic age in which we tend to dream of individual success, achievement, and prominence. That was not true in ancient times. All aspirations and dreams were for your family's success and prominence. The family was your primary identity, not your vocation, friendships and so on. It was the bearer of all hopes and dreams. Therefore there was nothing more important than to have and raise children who loved and honored you and who walked in your ways. In light of this, female 'barrenness' was considered the worse possible curse. A woman in this situation could not avoid feeling like a terrible failure."[2]

Though Keller wrote of women in ancient times who could not bear children, surely this applies to women who bore but later lost them.

Personal Take: What do we as a culture tend to look to for our primary source of identity? List as many as you can.

Keller's quote further helps us understand why Naomi told the women not to call her by her name anymore (v. 20).

Instead, she told them to call her _____, which means (circle one):

Bitter   Angry   Unforgiving   Depressed

Naomi made four statements that explain her request for a new name. Fill in the blanks below:

1. The _____ has made my life very bitter.

2. I went away full, but the _____ has brought me back empty.

3. Why call me Naomi? The _____ has afflicted me.

4. The _____ has brought misfortune upon me.

I realize this question has an obvious answer, but it's important to write it down. To whom did Naomi attribute her suffering?

A friend of mine has battled an illness for several years now. She's particularly young and beautiful, making her health problems all the more stark. A couple of nights ago she wrote me an e-mail that included a revealing phrase: "I can cope with the pain for the most part, but the despair of feeling forgotten by God's healing is overwhelming."

Does this not succinctly describe the deepest fear of the human soul—this sense of being forgotten by God, or possibly worse, that our suffering could be a direct blow from His hand? In one sentence my friend cut to the root of some of my greatest unease: me, unable to reconcile my suffering and the suffering of others with a very good God whose love endures forever. And in today's text we see Naomi erupt with the same agonizing despair that charges God with not just oversight of her pain but also with responsibility for it, "The Almighty has done this to me!"

Naomi stated this four different ways. I can't emphasize enough how important her words are. Please don't miss that she is a woman who is part of God's chosen family, who not only feels forsaken by God but utterly attacked by Him as well! I too have felt this way at different times in my life, when it seemed as if God was out to crush my every move. I got so frustrated by this notion at one point in college that I punched my steering wheel, causing the horn to eject from its socket and pulse up and down, hanging by a large spring. This made me even madder! Which is one reason I so appreciate that God did not edit Naomi's highly charged accusations out of the text, as they're not exactly proper, Sunday morning fare. I wouldn't quite know what to do with someone this honest on the front row of church except to perhaps offer a tissue and then run down the aisle screaming something like "ichabod!" But Naomi is certainly not the first to feel this way.

Read the following verses from Job and Psalms. Next to each verse describe the writer's suffering and how he saw God in it.

1. Job 9:16-19 _____

2. Job 10:8-9 _____

3. Job 19:8-10 _____

4. Psalm 22:1-2 _____

5. Psalm 88:6-8 _____

This is a profoundly important place for us to pause. I believe many Christian women are not nearly this honest with God or themselves. We feel forsaken by God or deep down we are angry or bitter with Him, but we never let ourselves stop long enough to address our feelings with Him. When our buried questions begin to percolate, we'd just as soon numb them by watching TV, updating our Facebook status (because, really, how will everyone survive if they don't know that "Kelly is eating gingersnaps right now"?), reading, napping, making a business call … anything to avoid sitting before the Lord.

Perhaps we're afraid of what we'll experience when we get there. Maybe we're fearful that we won't hear anything from God, that He'll require something of us we don't want to give, or that we'll learn something about ourselves we don't want to know. Perhaps it's too much work. Or maybe we fear coming unleashed like Naomi.

Regardless of your fears, I invite you to sit before the Lord in the true state of your heart (anger, fear, grief, questions, doubt, numbness, unbelief, and so forth). Please don't gloss over this part. Believe me, I'm just like you—I love the days of study where I get to fill in blanks and jot down correct answers because it doesn't require much of my heart but makes me feel good as one who has done her spiritual duty for the day. But God doesn't want our "right answers"; He wants our hearts … even if they're a little explosive like Naomi's.

> **Personal Prayer:** Read Hannah's prayers (1 Sam. 1:10-11,15-16), and then take a moment to be honest with yourself and with God. Sit quietly before Him with your questions and state of your heart. If you happen to be in a peaceful place with Him, stop and thank Him for this gift of a place of rest.

God doesn't want our "right answers"; He wants our hearts.

DAY 02 ARRIVING
A HOPEFUL GLIMMER

As we close the first chapter of Ruth, our story has narrowed pretty significantly. What began with six characters—Elimilech, Naomi, Mahlon, Kilion, Ruth, and Orpah—has quickly reduced to two unlikely protagonists, Naomi and Ruth. I say quickly because we can read the first chapter in a couple of minutes, potentially hindering us from giving proper weight to the famine, the move, the marriage of two sons, the death of a husband, the death of two sons, the beginning of a return journey, the turning back of one woman, and now the arrival in Bethlehem. There's a staggering amount going on here. It can be easy to miss the events' gravity because of the author's economy of words.

His approach reminds me of my sister, Megan, who sat down at the tender age of 10 to pen her first novel, *Why Don't You Like Me Aunt Bess?* Please enjoy the opening line: "Jane went to live with her Aunt Bess because her parents were killed on the way to a potluck."

Why tarry with needless and encumbering details when you can cut right to the chase? I understand Megan's urgency: She had a story to tell, but first she had to explain to the reader why Jane was living with her aunt (who apparently didn't like her). Not wanting to spend a lot of time on an explanation, she realized she needed to get rid of the parents quickly and humanely. So, great idea! Why not pick them off in a car accident on the way to a potluck? Our family *loves* this story!

I'm not suggesting the author of Ruth was mindlessly rushing through the details of the first chapter. However, I do think he was anxious to get to a very important story of redemption that he couldn't tell without first giving the essential background. So today we'll finish this chapter as the narrator begins to close it both literally and figuratively, while leaving us with the subtle hint that maybe—just maybe—our story is about to take a hopeful turn.

> Reread chapter 1 of Ruth in an uninterrupted setting. What especially stands out to you after looking at it as a whole? In verse 22, what new title did the narrator give Ruth?

Why do you think Scripture highlights Ruth's nationality now?

Read the last verse of chapter 1 and fill in the blanks.

Ruth and Naomi arrived in Bethlehem as the _____ _____ was beginning.

After all this immense hardship and suffering, we get the slightest glimpse that perhaps God was working something out for Naomi after all—that He had long been working behind the scenes, under the soil, and now His goodness was cropping up just above the ground as the barley harvest was beginning. Though it's still too early in the story to get our hopes up, I love this quote by Hubbard, "When God is at work, bitter hopelessness can be the beginning of some surprising good."[3]

Ecclesiastes 3:11
He has made everything beautiful in its time. He has also set eternity in the hearts of men; yet they cannot fathom what God has done from beginning to end.

Personal Response: Have you prayed or waited for something for a long season? If so, have you seen a glimpse—no matter how small—that God is working? Write about it below.

The notion of the beginning of barley harvest may not throw a chill up your spine like it might have for ancient readers, but we gather from this picture the assurance of provision. With each grain of barley we see opportunity, sustenance, hope, and a reminder that God's timing is perfect. He brought them back to Bethlehem just as harvest began.

Because Ruth and Naomi's story up to this point literally hinges on verse 22 and because Scripture has so much to say about harvests, I want to survey some verses outside the Book of Ruth. And in case you're wondering if any of this harvest-talk applies to you, the unique thing about harvests is that if you've got one you need to start hauling it in, and if you don't, it would be good to start throwing out some seed. Either way, the concept of harvesting always applies, it's just a matter of what side of it you're on—sowing or reaping. (And, by the way, both are good and necessary seasons of life.)

Are you in a season of sowing, reaping, or both? Explain your answer here.

Read Genesis 8:22. How long will seedtime and harvest endure?

Read Exodus 34:21. True/False: According to Old Testament law, one should rest on the seventh day during the plowing season but not during harvest.

Read Leviticus 23:9-14. According to the law, what were the Israelites to do with the first grain of their harvest?

How can we apply this principle in our modern lives? (Try to think beyond the simple answer of tithing.)

Read Jeremiah 5:24. True/False: The people to whom Jeremiah prophesied feared and acknowledged God as the One who provided their harvest.

It's hard for us to appreciate these concepts. At least it is for me. The closest I come to any of this is on Wednesday mornings when I pick up my produce and meat box from a truck that delivers from a local farm. It's an organic, green, free-range type thing that Lauri turned me onto one night while the "nogs" sat around on her porch eating fresh strawberries. Those little berries cost me a year's subscription to a local farm for weekly deliveries of fresh produce and an assortment of meats I now can't resist. And I was so content with pesticides and hormones before. You'd be amazed at how scrawny a nonhormon-pumped chicken is, by the way. I am now not beneath mining for meat in previously forbidden territories (so sorry to my many vegetarian friends).

My point is that I seldom thought about farming until last year when my local farm sent e-mails that included statements like: "No eggs this week because the chickens won't lay in this heat," "The price of honey is going up because bees are mysteriously disappearing," "Tomatoes are looking incredible," or "Would anyone like a sugar-cured pork jowl?" *Not really.* What's a jowl?

Though I still don't get all that close to the process, I newly appreciate what it means to depend on God's grace to water the soil, bring the sun, and keep all the symbiotic relationships going while sustaining

nogs or nog girls: women who gathered to study *No Other Gods* and got stuck with the name.

the farmers' health. It is a good reminder of God's precision. All good things come from His hand, whether we get our food straight from the ground or polished from the supermarket. It is all from Him.

Since we've looked at a few biblical references regarding the physical process of harvesting, I can't help but look at the process that affects most of us much more tangibly—the spiritual process of sowing and reaping. I can't think of a better passage than the emotional metaphor of harvest the psalmist paints of the believer's pilgrimage.

> **Read Psalm 126:1-6, keeping in mind that it's written from the perspective of Israelite exiles returning home from Babylon (much like Naomi returning home from Moab).**

> **What action often comes before reaping with songs of joy (v. 5)?**

> **What will our weeping and our seed turn to (v. 6)?**

The "nogs" helped me edit this study. When we got to this point, Anadara said, "Hey, this is one of my favorite psalms. Where's my personal response moment?" So here's her personally written question for you:

> **Personal Response: Practically speaking, how can you sow in your weeping?**

All good things come from His hand.

Every time I read this passage, I am reminded that it is not our weeping that brings the harvest but our sowing. We can grieve and shed an ocean of tears, but no harvest will come unless we simultaneously cast our seed. This is not easy, as difficult seasons generally do not motivate me to yell, "Put me in, Coach!" But as we learned in last week's study of Ruth and Orpah, what we do *while* we're weeping makes the difference.

It is not our weeping that brings the harvest but our sowing.

In closing today, note this wonderful truth: "Let us not become weary in doing good, for at the *proper time* we will reap a harvest if we do not give up" (Gal. 6:9, emphasis mine).

Could you use a glimpse of God breaking through the long barren land of a certain season? Do not give up, keep sowing. At just the right time the barley harvest will begin, and you'll just *so happen* to be arriving.

MY PORTION, YOU WILL EVER BE

Kelly Minter
See the story behind the song at www.livingroomseries.com.

As long as the sun blazes and burns
Your mercies will never fail
As long as the seedtime and harvest endure
Your mercies will never fail
When my soul is downcast within
Your compassions have no end

Chorus
Though the arrows pierce me
Though the darkness rages fiercely
You will be my stay
Though the earth gives way
My portion, You will ever be

With fear or with faith I'll say to my soul
Your mercies will never fail
A promise for ages, an anchor that holds
Your mercies will never fail
When my soul is downcast within
Your compassions have no end

Bridge
All because of Your great love
We are not consumed
All because of Your great love
Your mercies are ever new

Chorus

Kelly Minter. Mintyfresh Music (ASCAP)

To purchase this song or CD go to
www.LifeWay.com/livingroomseries.

DAY 03 ARRIVING
A MYSTERIOUS RELATIVE

If this story were a movie, you'd be about 35 minutes in—right about the place where you start committing to the story line and characters. This is where you start asking yourself things like, *Am I hooked, or is it the popcorn keeping me here?* It's where you begin to suspend reality and bond to the existing characters, not at all ready for that sudden appearance of the suspicious looking person who is about to change absolutely everything. But, of course, if the new mysterious character is a knight-in-shining-armor type, you could probably go along with it if someone were to throw in another, say, Diet Coke˚. Enter Boaz.

Today we begin a new chapter. Read Ruth 2:1-3.

We're going to take these verses one by one because each is so important in history and meaning. Prepare for a little Bible flipping and some slightly more technical information to better understand what's transpiring as the curtain opens on chapter 2. The surrounding details will prove important later, so stay engaged.

Verse 1. Because Ruth's story is part of the much larger story of God's ongoing redemptive plan, it's important to understand who this new individual is, where he comes from, and how he's related to the other prominent characters.

From what clan (some Bibles say *family*) was Boaz?

Perez   Judah   David   Elimilech

You'll remember from session I that Elimilech, Naomi, and their two sons came from Bethlehem-Judah, part of the nation of Israel. Israel was divided into 12 tribes, which began with the 12 sons of Jacob. One of the most significant is the tribe of Judah which we will later discover included Elimilech. This may seem extraneous now, but its importance becomes paramount as history unfolds; so hang onto this information.

Fill in the following: Boaz is from the nation of _____, the tribe of _____, and the clan/family of _____

A clan was a subgroup of a tribe consisting of several families. So what we're told in verse 1 is that Naomi had a significant relative named Boaz from her husband's clan. From a modern, western perspective this might make us think, *Oh good, Naomi's got a place to spend the holidays. Phew!* But for an Israelite of the day, "This small detail raises the interest and hopes of the readers, especially those who are familiar with Israelite family law and custom."[4] The fact that Naomi had a male relative from her husband's side of the family ushers in the first real sign that someone's alive who might be able to help. But we'll expound upon this more in future days. For now, just know that Boaz's relation to Naomi is significant beyond turkey dinners and "It's A Wonderful Life" reruns (but you knew that already …).

Now that we know who Boaz is from a perspective of lineage and nationality, describe what we're told about him as a person.

This is one of those times where digging a little deeper into the original language gives us a richer picture. The Hebrew term for "man of standing" is *gibbor hayil,* which most often means "war hero," "capable person," "wealthy man" (I've been looking for this guy all my life). But since it doesn't seem that Boaz had any military background, the term basically means "high social standing." In short, he was a powerful person—someone whose wealth and high reputation in Bethlehem gave him strong influence among his peers.

Verse 2. Immediately verse 2 skips to Ruth asking Naomi if she could go to the fields to pick up the leftover grain. At the moment this seems to have no apparent relation to its preceding verse, but it will connect for us soon. Right now we see that again the narrator used the title "Ruth the Moabitess." Notice what the author seemed to be doing: While Ruth resided in Moab he referred to her as Ruth, but upon her arrival in Bethlehem he twice called her Ruth the Moabitess. It seems the narrator was going out of his way to further highlight how unlikely any success would be as one coming from a land totally hostile to Israel as a nation, as well as her God. "Moabitess" is the condemning tag that could forever be her downfall, the piece of information that gnaws at her heels, that ruins her chances of ever becoming someone in Israel. In short, it's a tarnished heritage she is powerless to change.

Personal Take: Are there things about your own history or your family's history that haunt you in your quietest moments, that make you think God can never really love or use you? (Be as honest with your answer as you can).

I want you to see that God's tender heart for the outcast—or the one who feels unworthy—was expressed all the way back in Old Testament law. We think of such acceptance beginning with Christ, but really it was fulfilled in Him; God has always been concerned about the lowly, the poor, the outsider. If we didn't understand this about God's heart, we might think it odd for Ruth to have been given the liberty of gleaning from a field in Bethlehem Judah.

> God's tender heart for the outcast—or the one who feels unworthy—was expressed all the way back in Old Testament law.

> **Read Leviticus 19:9-10; 23:22; and Deuteronomy 24:19-22 and describe the Old Testament law pertaining to landowners and how this law affected Ruth's right to glean.**

> **What do these laws tell us about God's heart for the poor, foreigner, and widow?**

Although this law should have been well followed, Ruth stated that she hoped to find someone in whose eyes she could find favor. This may mean she was unfamiliar with Jewish law, or it may simply mean that because God's people don't always hold to His commands she was hoping for someone who would actually honor God's law of allowing a foreigner to glean. It's very possible that there were selfish and hostile landowners who wouldn't have wanted a widowed, Moabite woman on their land. Either way, Ruth was looking for someone gracious.

Verse 3. Most Bible translations say Ruth "went out and began to glean in the fields behind the harvesters." I'm not sure if gleaning apples is an actual thing or not, but it's the closest experience I've got, so I feel compelled to use it. When I was growing up, my parents used to take us apple picking every October. My dad was big on training us in integrity, so the apple orchard held a host of teaching moments. He would remind us to only eat the apples that were already on the ground, while all the ones we picked off the tree had to be put in the bag to later be weighed and paid for. Incidentally, this did not mean we could shake a tree to produce more ground-lying apples. That was the first thing I tried every year even though I don't even really like apples that much. To this day I think it was my dad's law producing sin in me (a "hilarious" Rom. 7:8 joke).

> **For Discussion: Do you have any gleaning experiences? (They don't necessarily have to be farming or field related.) Write just enough to remind you how you want to share your experience with your group.**

Carrie lamented about having to glean from her older sister's wardrobe when she was growing up. Yes, we love gleaning wisdom and insight from people we respect, but our sister's leg-warmers from the 80's, not so much. The perk for Carrie was that her mom felt guilty so she let her get her ears pierced early. Love it!

It's hard enough having to glean for ourselves, but I find Ruth's outstanding work ethic compelling, as she was unwilling for any time to pass before asserting herself for the benefit of her and Naomi's livelihood. Ruth was probably more motivated by wanting to provide for Naomi than even herself. We'll eventually come back to this important quality of hard work, but for now I want to look at one of the most fascinating turn of events in this story.

> **Verse 3 says, "As it turned out," Ruth happened to find herself working in whose field?**

> **Personal Take: In this context, how does the phrase "as it turned out" or just so "happened" strike you? Mark your reaction on the line below. (Translations differ. Just mark what's closest.)**

> |_____|_____|
> Divine Orchestration   Coincidence   Total Luck

Surprisingly enough, this phrase in Hebrew means that Ruth's chance chanced upon Boaz's field. It's a purposefully redundant phrase that literally means "a stroke of luck." [5] Of course if you made your mark near the Divine Orchestration slash on the spectrum, you're still as spiritual as you thought you were. The writer is employing an effective technique where he wants the reader to realize that Ruth stumbling upon the field of Boaz is more than just casual coincidence. He wants us to sit up and say, "Wait just a minute here, this can't just be luck!" He's prompting us to start noticing the invisible hand of Yahweh.

Yahweh:
the Hebrew name for the God of the Covenant

Though God's hand of providence is clearly at work here, how did Ruth's work ethic set her up for such a divine blessing?

Personal Response: Can you think of a time when you were faithfully going about a routine task or job and you had an "as it turned out" experience? If you have one, share the experience with your small group.

Even though we've only looked at three verses today, we've covered a lot of ground. It is my hope that we walk away with a heightened sense of what God is doing all around us, even in the seemingly mundane; and that we remember how purposeful He is, how intently He carves our paths, authors each stroke, and weaves our courses into others' lives.

God carves our paths, authors each stroke, and weaves our courses into others' lives.

As Elizabeth Barrett Browning put it,

"Earth's crammed with heaven, and every common
        bush afire with God;
But only he who sees, takes off his shoes, the rest
        sit round it and pluck blackberries, and
        daub their natural faces unaware."[6]

I don't want to miss the divine for the blackberries. Oh Lord, give me eyes to see!

DAY 04 ARRIVING
A DAY'S WORK

After I taught at a women's retreat last fall, someone asked me, "How do you see the things you see in Scripture?" Because I often feel like I don't see nearly enough, and because I really hadn't thought about it that way, I wasn't sure how to respond. But later I realized a few things that might be helpful as we study the Book of Ruth.

First, I almost always see something special in a passage of the Bible when I come to God desperate. Approaching the Word hungry is important because we're less likely to leave until we've been filled. Plus, God is close to the humble and delights in revealing Himself to those who know they need Him.

Second, I look for things, phrases, and descriptions—whatever might make me think more intently about what's happening in my reading.

Third, I try to relate what I'm reading to my life and the lives around me. As long as I see Scripture as historically and culturally out of touch, it will be difficult for me to understand its impact for today. This doesn't mean that I try to make the Bible all about me. Rather, I try to look for the heart behind its message so I can have impact in the here and now.

Fourth, and I could have put this first, I ask the Holy Spirit to open my eyes to see what I could never see on my own.

> **Given these things, read Ruth 2:4-7 and write any phrases, words, or descriptions that are meaningful to you.**

Two especially meaningful words to me are in verse 4, "Just then" Boaz arrived from Bethlehem (NIV). Some translations say, "Now behold" or "Later when." I like "just then" because it gives us that sense of another orchestration of God's providence coming into play. After having read that Ruth returned to Bethlehem just as the barley harvest was beginning and then reading "as it turned out" she happened to find herself working in Boaz's field, I just couldn't dismiss that "just then" Boaz happened to arrive exactly where Ruth was working.

We touched on God's providence yesterday, but here is another instance of His hidden hand expressing itself in the timing of Boaz and Ruth's first encounter. Perhaps this all means more to me since I've recently been contemplating God's specific orchestration in my life over the past several years. My memory doesn't have to stretch too far back to resurrect images of relational heartache, financial strain, career disappointment, and a general sense of having no idea where I was going. Yet I am just now far enough removed to see that God's divine hand was active in all my unknowing and confusion, threading together every heartbreak and triumph, never wasting a swatch, working all things together for good in the way that only God can.

When you walk through the dark, these things can seem mysterious and God distant. Until you have a "just then" moment when Yahweh suddenly passes through the curtain, and you begin to recognize that not only is He suddenly there but also that He has never left.

> **Personal Response:** Write a specific example of God's providence in your life that you couldn't necessarily see at the time.

We're not told why, but when Boaz noticed Ruth, he was intrigued and asked his foreman whose young woman she was. He probably recognized her as out of place among his workers and in his fields.

> **According to verse 6, the foreman described her familial and cultural heritage and also her work ethic. Fill in both aspects of his report to Boaz :**
>
> **heritage:**
>
> **work ethic:**

Although Boaz only asked to whom she belonged, I like that the foreman insisted on offering more than mere biological data, as if to say to Boaz, "She's a Moabitess who came back with Naomi, but what's really impressive is how incredibly hard-working she is, how she's gleaned nonstop from morning till now, except for this one tiny rest in the shelter!" The foreman reminds us that where we come from and what kind of blood runs through our veins is not nearly as impactful as our character and reputation.

Where we come from and what kind of blood runs through our veins is not nearly as impactful as our character and reputation.

According to Proverbs 22:1, what is more desirable than riches and more esteemed than silver or gold? (Circle your answer.)

an impressive pedigree   how many children you have
a good name   a humble spirit

Ruth was making a name for herself through her astounding hard work and determination in the fields. She wasn't afraid to slide up her sleeves and sweat with the boys. Not to mention in a territory that was foreign and in some cases dangerous. Ruth's pluck and fortitude make me want to leap out of the stands with my fists in the air for her. I'm a huge fan. She's simply inspiring! But she's also deeply convicting.

I so fear sounding like a full-fledged adult here, but I do think the ethic of hard work is being somewhat lost in our culture. So much of what we value tends to hinge on credit and "right now" and instant gratification, while having to really exert effort for something—that might not come till later—feels so laborious and passé. I just got off the phone with someone who was already broke and just charged $15,000 of nonessential items to her credit card in hopes that she can pay it off when she's back on her feet. Working hard for the $15,000, methodically saving, and waiting to make purchases is out of the question for her, especially since she can get what she wants now.

> **The ethic of hard work is being somewhat lost in our culture.**

Personal Response: Look back at verses 6-7. What impresses you most about Ruth's work ethic?

Read the following verses about work, and briefly sum up each message in your own words.

Ecclesiastes 9:10

Proverbs 14:23

54

Proverbs 22:29

Colossians 3:22-24

According to Genesis 2:15, God put Adam in the garden of Eden to work and take care of it.

> **Since the institution of work was in motion before Adam and Eve sinned, what does this tell us about God's creation of work?**

We can take much away from Ruth's outstanding work ethic. She saw no task as beneath her. She didn't let fear of the unknown or a foreign territory stop her. She sought out her work and didn't wait for it to come to her (v. 7, "please let me glean"). She worked "steadily from morning," getting up early and pacing herself—not trying to gather all her earnings in a get-rich-quick manner.

The Bible is clear about the blessings of steady hard work. Though trying, tedious, and exhausting at times, work not only brings blessing, it *is* the blessing. It also positions us in God's pathways. As we saw earlier, God's providence was all over Ruth's encounters, yet it was her obedience and work that placed her in the way of such providence. It's a mystery I don't fully understand, but it's an inspiring principle that we can embrace.

> **Work not only brings blessing, it *is* the blessing.**

I would be remiss if we didn't have a chance to personalize this message of work, as we're all affected differently. Some of us are workaholics—can we get a shout out for that "short rest in the shelter"? Even Ruth knew her limits. Some of us are on the opposite end of the spectrum, sitting around and waiting for the perfect job to drop in our laps. Ruth's example of going out and asking for opportunity really speaks to this. Others don't mind working but find themselves above certain jobs. Humbling themselves for menial tasks, like Ruth, seems out of the question. (I can't tell you how deeply it hurt me to learn this one.) Lastly, some of us are being stopped in areas of work by fear. Phew. … I love Ruth, but she kind of wore me out today.

Personal Response, Part 1: What's most convicting to you about today's study and why?

Personal Response, Part 2: How can you approach your work differently as a result of what's been meaningful to you?

DAY 05 ARRIVING
A FIRST ENCOUNTER

Today's bend in Ruth's story will not be nearly as hard on us as yesterday's. We can wipe the sweat from our brow and settle in for a much-anticipated conversation between Ruth and Boaz. There's nothing like capping off our week with a budding romance, friendship, or random meeting; we're not sure yet. But, hey, I'll take it any way it comes.

> **Thoughtfully read Ruth 2:8-9. Take in Boaz's very first words to Ruth, and list his instructions to her:**

> **Ruth hoped to pick up grain behind anyone showing her favor (see 2:2). How did Boaz's kindness exceed her highest hope?**

Ruth's unexpected blessings from Boaz remind me of Ephesians 3:20, which says that God is able to do more than all we can ask or imagine.

> **For Discussion: What's one thing God has done in your life that far exceeded what you could have asked for or dreamt of? Jot it down for discussion later.**

Ephesians 3:20
Now to him who is able to do immeasurably more than all we ask or imagine, according to his power that is at work within us.

In verse 9 Boaz says to Ruth, "Whenever you are thirsty, go and get a drink from the water jars the men have filled." At first glance this seems to be a simple act of kindness, but according to ancient customs, Boaz has just made an extraordinary offer.

> **Read Genesis 24:11,13; Deuteronomy 29:11; and John 2:7. What two types of people were drawing water?**

> _____ and _____

"What an interesting touch: a foreign woman who customarily would draw water *for* Israelites was welcome to drink water drawn *by* Israelites."[7] Not to mention that drawing the water more than likely took place at the gates of Bethlehem and then had to be carried to the fields. The sheer time and energy involved were significant, making Boaz's offer for Ruth to drink freely even more valuable.

> **Personal Response: Briefly write about a time when someone treated you with excessive kindness or generosity.**

Not only do we see Boaz providing for Ruth, but we also see him taking a stand to protect her. This is one of the most attractive things a man can do, wielding his strength and stature for the vulnerable. Verse 9 says Boaz ordered his men not to touch Ruth, this expression meaning, "to strike, harass, take advantage of, or mistreat."[8] One commentator said, "Boaz is hereby instituting the first anti-sexual-harassment policy in the workplace recorded in the Bible."[9] In essence, Boaz was showing Ruth—the foreigner, the lowly, the poor—*hesed,* by protecting the innocence of someone he didn't have to notice, much less provide for.

> **Write your own definition of *hesed*. (Hint: see p. 20.)**

I've been reading through Matthew, and I saw something that reminded me of Boaz and Ruth that I want you to see too.

> **Look for similarities in Matthew 12:1-8 and Ruth 2:8-9.**

> **In what distinct setting were Jesus and His disciples when the Pharisees accused them (v. 1)?**

> **True/False: The Pharisees cited the disciples for working on the Sabbath, a violation of Jewish law.**

Perhaps it was the now familiar location of a harvest field that caught my attention in Matthew 12. How interesting that the Pharisees went after Jesus and His disciples in a grain field, the very setting where Boaz committed to protecting Ruth. But what really caught my attention was the end of Jesus' recorded response to the Pharisees (vv. 7-8).

If the Pharisees had understood that Jesus desired mercy and not sacrifice, what would they not have done (v. 7b)?

Just as I was moved by Boaz's strong protection of Ruth's innocence, I was moved by Jesus' similar protection of His disciples. Even though I've seen this passage from other vantage points, I never noticed Jesus' strong reaction to the Pharisees as being from one who would not stand for His dearly loved followers to be falsely accused. You can almost hear Him say, "Back away from My people!" in their defense.

Personal Response, Part 1: Briefly write about a time when you defended or protected someone in a vulnerable position.

Personal Response, Part 2: This may be harder to define, but have you ever experienced God defending or protecting you? If so, write about it here.

Perhaps after reading the accounts in Ruth and Matthew you're thinking, *That's great for Ruth and the disciples, but I'm not innocent. I don't qualify to be protected like that. My history is too blemished. I'm not worth that kind of care.* If this is your tendency, let's first recall that Ruth's ethnic background did not endear her to Boaz's lavish treatment. She was a most unlikely candidate for exceptional treatment. And most of the disciples didn't fare much better, as some came straight out of deceptive lifestyles when Jesus called them. Both accounts are pictures of grace where it could never have been earned.

Grace
Undeserved acceptance and love received from another, especially the characteristic attitude of God in providing salvation for sinners.

In keeping with this beautiful truth, meditate on Romans 5:6-8.

Through Jesus we are made innocent.

May the gospel's truth silence every accusing voice and erase every guilty thought. Through Jesus we are made innocent.

Today's readings are particularly meaningful to me, as one who is especially pained by powerful accusers who prowl in the fields, stalking the innocent and vulnerable. In the Book of Ruth we saw that Boaz forbade it, and in the Book of Matthew we saw that Jesus rebuked it. I am encouraged that these two examples in Scripture, among so many others, reveal the heart of God toward the vulnerable. We've seen the beginning of Boaz's lavish treatment of Ruth, but we have only begun to discover the well of his kindness.

ARRIVING

Kelly Minter
See the story behind the song at www.livingroomseries.com.

I packed my bags and hit the road
I left that town with all its ghosts
And it's been the longest winding way home

I never thought I'd ever leave
Now I'm somewhere in the in-between
Yesterday's lost its grip on tomorrow

Chorus
I'm arriving, I'm arriving
It's been a long time coming
The horizon, the horizon
Is close enough to touch
And I'll be there real soon

I've shed my comforts like a cloak
Can't get ahead with a heavy load
I've let go for the promise before me

Chorus

Bridge
I didn't know if I'd ever make it
I didn't know if my heart could take it
But I'm standing here on the edge of where I belong
I'm gonna walk right through these gates
Tired but wide awake
Cause the old is giving way to the new

Kelly Minter
Mintyfresh Music (ASCAP)

FRESH TOMATO PASTA
SERVES 6

I talk about this recipe in the introduction to week 4. It's an easy, personal, fresh, and healthy favorite.

1 (12 oz.) package dried linguine
4 large tomatoes, chopped
5 cloves garlic, minced (I like tons of garlic; you can back this off.)
6 big leaves of fresh basil, chopped
3 tablespoons olive oil
½ teaspoon salt
¼ teaspoon freshly ground pepper
1 (2¼ oz.) can sliced ripe olives, drained
1 cup crumbled feta cheese

Directions
The above measurements are good starters, but feel free to add more or less to taste. Cook pasta according to package directions. (If you're really feeling inspired, make your own pasta. All you need is semolina flour, eggs, and olive oil. You can find a recipe anywhere on the Web.) OK, if this is too much, just buy it from the store.

While pasta water is boiling, combine tomatoes and next 5 ingredients. Salt the mixture and let the tomatoes soak up the salt for a few minutes, this will bring out the flavor of the tomatoes. (If heirloom tomatoes are in season, they work great.) Drain pasta, and place in a large bowl. Top with tomato mixture, and sprinkle with olives and cheese.

PARMESAN FLATBREAD
PRE-HEAT OVEN TO 475° SERVES 6

Without fancy bakeware, you can make amazing flatbread. The girls ate it up.

1 teaspoon white sugar
1 (.25 oz.) package active dry yeast
⅓ cup warm water
2 cups all-purpose flour
2 tablespoons olive oil
¼ teaspoon salt
¼ cup grated fresh or pre-grated parmesan

Directions
Dissolve sugar and yeast in warm water in a small bowl. Let stand until creamy, about 10 minutes. In a larger bowl, combine the yeast mixture with flour. Stir in additional water, one tablespoon at a time, until all of the flour is absorbed. When the dough has come together, knead it on a lightly floured surface for a couple of minutes.

Lightly oil a bowl. Place the dough in the bowl and turn to coat. Cover with a damp cloth and let rise in a warm place for about 30 minutes or until double in size. Preheat oven to 475°.

Punch the dough down and turn it out onto a lightly floured surface; knead briefly. Pat or roll the dough into a sheet and place on a lightly greased baking sheet (I like either a stone or the kind with holes in it). Brush the dough with oil; sprinkle with salt and lightly dust with parmesan to taste.

Bake 10 to 20 minutes, depending on desired crispness. Moist and fluffy is less time, crispy a little longer. Let cool for 5 minutes. Cut into 1½" strips with a pizza cutter. Then cut strips in half. They will look like little bread sticks.

For an easy dip for the bread, combine desired amount of olive oil, balsamic vinegar, and freshly grated parmesan in a serving bowl.

I JUST GOT BACK FROM TAKING MY FRIEND, LISA, TO SEE HER PROBATION OFFICER. THOUGH ALCOHOL WAS HER PREFERRED DRUG FOR ABOUT 23 YEARS, SHE WILL SOON HAVE GONE A FULL YEAR WITHOUT A DROP. I MET HER AT "THE NEXT DOOR." SOMETHING ABOUT HER SPIRIT HIDING BEHIND HER BLOODSHOT EYES MADE ME KNOW SHE WAS TENTATIVELY HOPEFUL THAT PERHAPS, THIS TIME, SHE WOULD KICK ALCOHOLISM FOR GOOD. SINCE THAT FIRST MEETING, LISA GRADUATED THE PROGRAM, BECAME A CHEF, PAYS RENT, TAKES A CULINARY CLASS, AND DRINKS A LOT OF THINGS LIKE COFFEE AND SPRITE.

This is all the good part; the tricky piece is wading through the tangled consequences of 23 years of alcoholism. Things like debt, lost work opportunities, a couple of wrecked cars, broken relationships, an invalid driver's license, and long drives to the probation officer. This doesn't leave a lot of reserve for things like a cracked tooth wiping out her emergency fund, her boyfriend breaking up with her, or her roommate unexpectedly leaving her with the rent due. These are the times when even the slightest act of kindness and generosity helps Lisa refrain from reaching out for the false savior of alcohol.

During our drive to the courthouse, I realized there are certain things about the justice system I respect but don't fully understand. Like, how is someone without a license supposed to transport herself to a courthouse that's an hour away in a city with no public transportation? This is where my valid driver's license came in handy, though my friends rarely let me enjoy its benefits when traveling with me. Lisa, on the other hand, had no such luxury. Poor thing probably wished she had skate boarded.

Second thing I don't understand about the justice system is token arrests. On our way to the courthouse, Lisa casually mentioned that when we got there she'd be getting arrested. This made me pull off at the nearest Dunkin' Donuts® because—doggone it—if you know you're about to get arrested, my mantra has always been to at least treat yourself to coffee and a slew of donut holes. 'Cause let's face it, the day's on its way down from here.

"You're getting arrested? How long is this going to take? Are we going to jail?" These were the questions I asked while spreading cream cheese onto my bagel. Lisa tried to explain it was mostly a formality. Since by God's grace I haven't gone through a real—or fake—arrest, I was a little lost. Either way, I still felt really good about the donuts and bagels; an arrest is something you don't want to go through hungry.

After sitting in the holding room with some rough-looking characters for what felt like a year at the DMV, Lisa was called. I stood outside the door as she nervously sat in front of the black metal desk, appropriately in front of a cinder block wall. The officer appeared stern, accentuated by his badges and earpiece. I don't know if I've ever met a probation officer before, but he was everything I'd ever imagined one to be: balding, slightly pudgy, mustache, and all. None of this seemed especially good.

When Lisa emerged, I was anxious for the outcome. Like, how did the arrest go? She surprised me by emphasizing how nice he was. Apparently, he asked if she was staying sober and she proudly responded, "One year!" He glanced up, smiled slightly, and quietly said, "Thirty-three for me … just so you know, it can be done."

Lisa left with a noticeably lighter load, fueled by the seemingly small kindness and encouragement of her officer. He had noticed her. Took time to single her out as an individual, not just another file or offender. Lisa could make it another day. And maybe that day would lead to another and another until she'd be able to say to a fellow struggler, "Thirty-three for me … just so you know, it can be done." Yes, kindness is a powerful thing.

I've repeatedly read the passage we're about to study this week, examining every word and action, looking for that special nugget to emerge from its pages. And, of course, it contains many such treasures; but in some ways I think I almost began to miss the overarching theme for its utter simplicity! With all its cultural differences and Hebrew grammatical complexities, this passage is very plainly about kindness: the kindness of Boaz to Ruth, which so perfectly builds upon the kindness of Ruth to Naomi. Overwhelming kindness. A lost art in a world that is often rushed, rude, and too busy for the concerns of others.

Last week we looked at some of the Old Testament laws in Deuteronomy and Leviticus, making us aware of God's mandate for His people to show kindness to the poor and foreigner. This week we'll see Boaz acting in accordance with God's heart of kindness, meaning we won't just be reading about an extraordinarily kind man but an extraordinarily kind God.

DAY 01 AN ENCOUNTER
UNEXPECTED KINDNESS

To refresh your memory, last week we closed in the middle of a conversation between Ruth and Boaz. We can either attribute this to extremely poor planning on my part or consider it an effective literary technique that whetted your appetite for the rest of their exchange. We concluded with Boaz's first words to Ruth, which included an offer to stay working in his field, protection from the men, and the gift of freely drinking the water the servants had drawn. Boaz's kindness toward Ruth sparks hopefulness in my heart about the power of kindness, especially the tender acts of kindness shown by a man to a woman. And if you're not married or romantically involved, this does not exclude you from such experiences. Boaz and Ruth were mere acquaintances when Boaz extended such graciousness to her.

As I write, I'm on a worship tour traveling on a tour bus with 14 people, 11 of them men. I say this merely to set the environment (smells, humor, and all). Most mornings when we wake up we make our way to the front lounge, one by one, vying for coffee, granola bars, and some semblance of breakfast. Today I noticed several guys had steaming bowls of oatmeal and honey that looked surprisingly good (but then again, stale pizza looked good to me the other night, so my references are a bit off). This made me start digging through the cabinets for the oats, when our bass player, Daniel, jumped up from the couch, offered me his seat and said in his South African vernacular, "Keh-lee, I will make it for you! I know the exact proportions." He started laughing at the monotony of being on a bus and said, "It will give me value!" When the timer went off a few minutes later, our drummer, Ben, beat me to the microwave, grabbed me a spoon, and handed me my bowl. I'm not sure there's anything more mundane than oatmeal, but today Daniel and Ben's kindness made it the best I've ever had.

Today we'll see how Ruth responded to the incredible kindness of Boaz and how he invoked Yahweh's blessing on her.

Read Ruth 2:10-12, noticing Ruth's dramatic response to Boaz. Why was Ruth so surprised by Boaz's favor (v. 10)?

www.livingroomseries.com Get a glimple of the "nogs" as they cook and chat in the kitchen. Then hear Kelly talk about how a life can be changed by kindness.

Keep the next exercise gender specific because, although the kindness between women is extraordinary, there's something unique about a man's kindness toward a woman. Also, it doesn't have to be limited to a romantic setting. Alli said how much it meant to her when her brother used to stand up for her.

For Discussion: Describe a time when you were overcome by a man's kindness.

Why did Boaz show Ruth such kindness (v. 11)?

Personal Response: In our culture men and women (stereotypically speaking) tend to notice one another for physical beauty, wealth, and social status. How do the reasons Boaz listed for noticing Ruth significantly differ from ours?

Boaz was impressed with Ruth for reasons that go beyond beauty, heritage, culture, status, and wealth.

I find verse 11 contains one of this story's more encouraging and hopeful elements. Boaz was impressed with Ruth for reasons that go beyond beauty, heritage, culture, status, and wealth. We cannot forget that Ruth was a foreign woman from the enemy land of Moab with no husband, children, money, or elite status. Yet one of the most powerful men in Bethlehem noticed her for something that transcends culture, beauty, and riches—her character. This is staggeringly countercultural: Her story circulated to the top, not because of her agent or publicist, but because of the *hesed* she showed her mother-in-law, her suffering through the loss of her husband, the courage to leave her homeland and family, and the bravery to plant roots with a people she didn't know.

I believe the Lord longs to honor such quiet and humble sacrifices, bringing such deeds to light when His timing allows. Much like Ruth taking care of Naomi, I think of my mom who has literally given up part of the last three years of her life to take care of my grandparents, my beloved Pop passing away just a few months ago. She has cooked, cleaned, waited in doctor's offices, talked to social security agents, bathed, blotted wounds, played cards, shuttled to church, hauled oxygen tanks, divvied pills, cried, perused the library for murder mysteries and autobiographies, pep-talked, folded laundry, played more cards … This enormous sacrifice is rarely noticed, though undoubtedly seen by God Himself.

> **Perhaps some of you have also been in long seasons of unnoticed hard work, sacrifice and faithfulness, wondering if your story will ever make it to the ears of a Boaz. Let the words of Isaiah 58:6-12 refresh you today.**
>
> **What does God promise for those who take care of their own flesh and blood, who feed the poor, help the oppressed, and fight against injustice (vv. 8-11)?**
>
> **Ruth 2:12 has to be one of the most warm and eloquent verses in all of Scripture. Slowly read it again and answer these questions:**
>
> **What other name besides LORD does Boaz call God?**
>
> **How is this name significant considering Ruth is a Moabitess?**

Ruth 2:12
May the LORD repay you for what you have done. May you be richly rewarded by the LORD, the God of Israel, under whose wings you have come to take refuge.

Many of us have been touched by the tender image of finding refuge under the wings of Almighty God. We can't forget that, physically speaking, it might have been easier for Ruth to have found refuge in the strong arms of Boaz. But as wonderful and powerful as Boaz was, he realized that only God could truly repay and reward her. Boaz could offer water, grain, and protection, but only God could pull off the much bigger blessing of reward and redemption. I find this overwhelmingly significant, confessing that looking to a person to solve my problems or give my life worth and meaning can be my first instinct. But, here, Boaz—among the most capable and resourced of men—knew his limitations; he knew that only God could truly redeem Ruth.

Scripture isn't clear about how Ruth came to take refuge under the wings of God. Surely she wasn't taught about Him as she grew up in Moab. Perhaps her husband Mahlon spoke about the God who ruled the people he had left behind in Bethlehem. Or maybe Naomi, before her bitter losses, told stories about the things He had done for them in days of old. We're not sure how Ruth came to know the God of Israel, but we know she was intent to follow Him before she ever got to Bethlehem. We know this from her illustrious speech to Naomi, "Your God will be my God."

Ruth is not the only one who has found shelter under the wings of Yahweh. Read these psalms and meditate on their meaning for you:

Psalm 36:7

Psalm 61:4

Psalm 91:1-16

For Discussion. How did you come to find refuge under the wings of God? Write a brief description below, taking a few moments to meditate on your own incredible story of being drawn into relationship with Jesus.

James
5:17

DAY 02 AN ENCOUNTER
HUMILITY

The idea of humility is an ebbing notion in today's culture where arrogance, perfection, and star power are prized, making it difficult for any of us to admit our true weaknesses. We are mostly taught to embellish our good sides and shroud our areas of struggle, and yet we see in Scripture that God dearly values those who are meek and lowly in spirit. So often I'm compelled to veil my weaknesses and cover my flaws, but how wonderful when I can honestly admit who I really am or what I'm really going through, especially within the realm of the church. Today Ruth will remind us that open honesty in the form of humility is a beautiful quality—even in a culture that exalts the image of having it all together.

Today I want to do something that I hope won't frustrate all the type-A personalities out there. If this is you, go mow your lawn or dust under your bed or something and then come back so you can feel like you've accomplished a task, because today we're going to focus on one half of one verse in the Book of Ruth. If you're highly driven, you'll be much less bugged this way.

> **Read Ruth 2:13. The second half of this verse finds Ruth stunned by the excessive kindness of Boaz, primarily because: (circle your answer)**

She was a Moabitess.   She was a widow.

She had less standing than servant girls.   She was a woman.

I remember being struck by this verse during a humbling time in my life. Ruth wasn't even at the level of the servant girls; she was actually *beneath* them. As if being a servant girl weren't low enough. At least they had some standing and rights, but Ruth didn't qualify as being one of them. To Ruth's utmost credit, here is a woman unashamed of her position and unafraid to keep pressing forward despite her lowly status. This was not about false humility or self-hatred but about being humble in its truest form—the kind that doesn't manipulate pity but freely and honestly expresses itself.

When I was in college, I had a sociology textbook that listed every known profession from most prestigious to most humbling. I can't remember what stood at the top, but I will never forget coming home and telling my dad that the number one most humbling job in the world was shoe shining. We were cracking up because right before my dad started the church he is still pastoring after 34 years, he gave golf lessons, and yes, shined people's shoes. My dad now realizes that those years of sitting at people's feet with a well-worn rag and pitch black polish was not all that far from what God was preparing him to do for the rest of his life—serve Christ's body. The Lord knew my dad needed to be humbled, not for the sake of hurting and humiliating him, but so the posture of his heart could be fully surrendered. And … so he would know how to handle success and notoriety when it came.

> Nothing prepares us for enormous blessing and impact like a season of humbling.

Maybe the Lord took Ruth on such a humbling journey because He knew the heights to which He would one day bring her. Nothing prepares us for enormous blessing and impact like a season of humbling (I believe I first heard this from Beth Moore's teaching). But this notion of humility is quite unpopular and hardly newsstand fare. I was reminded of this while perusing a magazine article about how to feel good—and who doesn't want to feel good? So I mined through its offerings expecting more asparagus recipes and yoga techniques, but the female columnist really surprised me with something profoundly less helpful: "I've learned that the key to living a wonderful life is this: If it doesn't make me feel good, I don't do it anymore."

What? Who does this woman's laundry, changes her kid's diapers? Does she work? Maybe she just hangs out with her friends, but friendships don't always feel good. Does she enjoy flossing? Reading this article suddenly made me feel not so good, so I took her advice and stopped (reading—not flossing). If only the "key" to a wonderful life were as simple as not doing what didn't feel good. This philosophy would have kept Ruth in Moab. Unless she naturally loved long journeys, bitter in-laws, and sweating for scraps. Seasons of hardship and humbling don't show up in the "how to feel good" articles, but let me appeal from the pages of Scripture that perhaps nothing is more beneficial for us in the long run.

No one was more entitled to live a feel-good life than Jesus Christ. And yet we read something very different about what He chose and what He calls us to choose.

According to Philippians 2:3-11, what are we encouraged to do (vv. 3-5)?

In what specific ways did Jesus display humility (vv. 6-8)?

Verse 9 starts off with the word "therefore," implying a significant shift. Because Jesus chose to humble Himself, God, *therefore,* chose to exalt Him to the highest place. Be encouraged that humbling seasons are for our ultimate benefit, though they are painful and, well, humbling. We will see this truth play out huge in Ruth's life, which is why we're spending a full day highlighting her incredibly low position. Things are about to change for her, but we won't appreciate the transformation without first noticing the depths in which she now resides.

The following verses are encouraging and hopeful to those of us who are willing to humble ourselves. Paraphrase each reference.

Matthew 23:11-12

James 4:6,10

1 Peter 5:5-6

You might be in a similar place where God is humbling you, leveling you to the place that feels below the lowest low. I am still limping from those days. Not at all to say that I've ever walked a road as tumultuous as Ruth's, but the Lord has definitely brought me through some painfully humbling times that stung, burned, and melted away the chill of pride. But just as the hollow of winter mysteriously gives rise to the bounty of spring, so times of humbling and hardship prepare us for a wealth of blessing we would have otherwise been unable to handle.

> Times of humbling and hardship prepare us for a wealth of blessing.

Personal Response: Does God have you in a season of humbling?

If so, how do these verses encourage you?

This topic of humility has been a lively one for the "nogs." Carrie wrote in the margin of today's study "wife." I think that's short for loving your husband and family is often thankless, invisible, and at times humbling, even though she has the best husband and son a girl could hope for. And Anadara talked about how easy it is to feel like you're behind or not where you're supposed to be when judging yourself by what bellows from the media. She told us she had been sick for a few days and had ended up watching more TV than normal, a natural remedy for the flu. But after such concentrated viewing she found herself feeling behind and not measuring up to the frenetic drive and pace of the characters on many of the shows where more, bigger, winner, beautiful, and wealthy are the prized themes.

After this realization she said a most penetrating thing in our group: "When it comes to my spiritual life, I feel more drawn than driven." She further explained that God does not create a frenzy of anxiousness within us where we're compelled to keep up, strive, and exist in a driven state to accomplish our own greatness. Instead, she described the quiet and peaceful process of God drawing us along in our journey. This resonated truth to me, so I had to share it with you.

For Discussion: In what ways does media contradict God's desire for us to be a humble people? In what ways does it support it?

When God has ordained the humbling, you can be wholly certain that His love is the catalyst.

As we close today, let me encourage you to not resist the process of humility. When God has ordained the humbling, you can be wholly certain that His love is the catalyst, and the process is forming in you a meek and gentle heart, preparing you for the abundance ahead. If God has you in the place of a servant girl—or even beneath one—humble yourself under His mighty hand. In due time He will lift you up.

"He raises the poor from the dust and lifts the needy from the ash heap; he seats them with princes, with the princes of their people. He settles the barren woman in her home as a happy mother of children. Praise the Lord" (Ps. 113:7-9).

DAY 3 AN ENCOUNTER
INVITED TO THE TABLE

Eighth grade, shop class, I made the coolest wooden clock. Circa 1980s. I'm feeling it might be worth something at the moment—if only I knew whose basement it was appreciating in. Only two other girls were in my class, but I couldn't be deterred when the chance to saw, sand, and stain were at stake. Seriously, what ever could be as compelling in home economics? No doubt some of my favorite moments of junior high took place around that colossal woodblock table, etched with every last initial of who-loved-who on the top and plastered with every flavor of gum underneath.

This must be why I love my dining room table so much—a redone shop table a friend of mine bought at a school auction for 60 bucks. She pulled off the janitor-green lockers, had me scrape off the assorted gum, sand and stain the top, secure honey-glazed wooden legs to the bottom, and bingo, an elegantly industrial dining room table big enough for the largest of gatherings. (OK, it was an enormous headache, but the end result was amazing.) With refined chairs and a vase of flowers juxtaposing its nicks and grooves, I like to think it welcomes the broken and bruised with an element of style. All are welcome at this humble table.

Maybe not everyone gives so much thought to their tables, but to me, communing and dining are at the essence of relationships. This may be why today's reading feels so remarkable to me.

> **To me, communing and dining are at the essence of relationships.**

Read Ruth 2:14.

We don't know how much time passed between yesterday's verse 13 and this verse when Boaz invited Ruth to a meal. And again, we can't overemphasize how extraordinary this invitation was and how far it exceeded what the law required. Suddenly, Ruth found herself sitting at Boaz's table, not among the gleaners, but among the reapers! This part of Ruth's story reminds me of King David and the astonishing kindness he showed to a young man named *Mephibosheth*. I want you to read it for yourself because the similarities are striking, and its message inspiring. (For a little background, this event took place after the death of Jonathan, King David's dearest friend.)

Read 2 Samuel 9:1-12 and list all the similarities you can find between Ruth's and Mephibosheth's stories. Be as specific and detailed as you can.

Personal Take: The narrator of Ruth went out of the way to remind us Ruth was a Moabitess, and the author of 2 Samuel reminded us several times that Mephibosheth was crippled in both feet. What is the purpose of highlighting these obstacles?

I believe we all deeply long to be invited "to the table." It represents all things that speak belonging, acceptance, and the honor of being chosen. It is a picture of intimacy, conversation, nourishment, and safety. What is more valuing than being invited to someone's table? Especially when the invitation is extended by someone highly esteemed like King David or Boaz.

> We all deeply long to be invited "to the table."

For Discussion: Have you ever considered it a remarkable honor to be invited to someone's table? Describe the details of the host, meal, ambience, and setting.

Part of what was remarkable about Ruth and Mephibosheth being invited to dine with nobility is that they were not considered worthy to be there. They had no entrance on their own, no right to the meal, no privilege to the table. This gift could only be extended by someone who not only had a heart of extraordinary kindness but also had the authority to do so. Kindness alone could never have been enough; power had to be part of the equation.

Only when the forces of power and kindness come together will we be in a position to eat from the King's table. We are to prepare for this meal now, but the One with the authority of God and the kindness of a Lamb, Jesus Christ Himself, will ultimately fulfill it in the heavenlies with every saint present. This is the most important feast we will ever be invited to.

I know we're jumping around a bit today, but I want you to read in Revelation about this remarkable gathering. Keep in mind that though stories like Mephibosheth's and Ruth's took place in time, space, and history, they also serve as pictures of spiritual realities.

> **Read what Revelation 19:6-10 says about this feast. According to verse 9, who is blessed?**

When getting married, regardless of the season, in- or outdoors, afternoon or evening, a bride always needs a gown. Incidentally, the wedding feast of the Lamb will prove no different.

> **What will we be wearing (vv. 7-8)?**

> **What do these garments stand for (v. 8)? (Circle your answer.)**

> **our cumulative Bible knowledge   the money we've tithed**

> **the righteous acts of the saints   the prayers of the righteous**

This very interesting passage says the church (the bride of Christ) has made herself ready by wearing fine linens that represent the righteousness (righteous acts) of the saints. At first glance, this almost looks like getting to Christ's table is a matter of living the best life we possibly can, shunning our sinful tendencies while bolstering our good deeds, and hoping that in the end our "outfit" will be white and clean enough to inherit heaven. But verse 8 indicates something entirely different:

> **Fill in the blank: "Fine linen, bright and clean, was _____ her to wear."**

I have heard the gospel message preached all my life, but suddenly I am relieved and rejoicing all over again. The linen has been given to us to wear! It is not up to us to clothe ourselves in our own self-righteousness any more than it was up to Mephibosheth to mend his feet or Ruth to redeem her heritage. Jesus Christ *is* our righteousness. The good news of the gospel is that Jesus has extended an invitation

> There is nothing that Christ does not have the power to forgive or that is too scarlet to be covered by the white linen of His righteousness.

to every one of us. I can almost hear the "but you don't know my past" sentiments resounding in some of your heads because the same voices have accused in mine. Please know that there is nothing that Christ does not have the power to forgive or that is too scarlet to be covered by the white linen of His righteousness. Though we are unworthy, we are invited to God's table because of Christ's kindness and authority.

Personal Response: You have been invited by Jesus Christ to dine at the King's table. If you've already accepted the linens of righteousness, write some words of thanks to Christ for such a remarkable gift. (Think of how Ruth and Mephibosheth might have thanked Boaz and David).

If this is a new truth that you've never understood in quite this way, today is the day to be clothed in Christ's righteousness. On page 174 there is a much broader explanation of what Jesus did for us. Please take time to read about His immeasurable love for you.

Like Mephibosheth, we are crippled in both feet; like Ruth, we bear the stain of Moab. Apart from Christ we are excluded from the right to dine at God's table. Ruth needed Boaz, Mephibosheth needed David, but we all need the Son of God.

Dearest Jesus, This is a gift too amazing to fathom, too lavish to take in. But like Ruth and Mephibosheth we gladly come to your table knowing that it is only because of You that we are invited. The power and kindness of Boaz and David were extraordinary, but even they had no power to forgive sins and no authority to clothe us in linens of righteousness. These gifts only come by the power of God through the kindness of Christ. We love You and thank You. Amen.

DAY 04 AN ENCOUNTER
A GENEROUS GIFT

OK, today's really good. That's all I've got for an opener. Get in there.

According to Ruth 2:15-19, how much grain did Ruth carry back to town?

3 pounds   1½ bushels   1 ephah   4 boxes

It's slightly unclear how much one ephah of barley was, but scholars suggest it's between 30 and 50 pounds. We can know for sure this was an astounding amount of grain to take home after only one day's work.

Why did Ruth have so much grain (vv. 15-16)?

Notice that the men helped supply Ruth with some of the sheaves by leaving them on the ground, but Ruth still had to do the work of picking them up. This is a poignant picture of how God provides us with the gift of work yet still invites us to do the work. This whole symbiotic relationship has been on my mind lately. Maybe it's because I'm self-employed and have gone through long seasons where work was slow yet have also enjoyed really over-the-top times of abundance. In the midst of pondering all this, I recently came across a passage that spoke to my heart and speaks to our story.

> God provides us with the gift of work yet still invites us to do the work.

Read 2 Corinthians 9:6-11.

This passage touches on many elements of sowing, reaping, giving, and caring for the poor; but I want to specifically look at one thing that relates to Boaz directing his foremen to leave barley for Ruth. Look at verse 10 and answer the following question:

Who supplies seed to the sower?

Even though the sower is out sowing, someone must provide him with the seed to cast in the first place. Even though Ruth was out gleaning, someone graced her with the sheaves to collect. If you are currently in a season of great abundance, I encourage you to passionately thank God that He has given you the seed to sow and the sheaves to gather. For most of us, it's easy to take for granted the fact that we have work, but what an enormous blessing that is! If you're struggling through a slow season of work, be encouraged that God will provide you with what you need. He is the One who gives seed to the sower and bread for food!

God will provide you with what you need.

List the steps involved in the process of arriving in the field and ending up with grain at the end of the day (vv. 17-18).

A lot of steps came between picking up some barley and ultimately getting it home in a form Ruth could actually use. I know a tiny bit about this because when I was in high school my dad got into breadmaking. Being the all-or-nothing guy he is, buying whole wheat flour at the store was not sufficient. Instead, he found some obscure outfit that sold him actual wheat berries. I remember my mom mentioning to him that she wouldn't know a wheat berry if it hit her in the head (translation: Have you lost your mind?).

And he couldn't just purchase a lunch bag or two of these marvels; he dragged them home in industrial-sized potato sacks that weighed more than punching bags. He kept them in our storage room because they took up the space of two more children and then transferred cups-full up the stairs, meticulously measured them into his commercial grade Vita-mix blender (the one that boasts the ability to grind two-by-fours in mere seconds), and out came that thing you can buy at the store—*wheat flour*. But why would you want to do that when you can go to all this trouble?

Once this simple step was accomplished, he began the bread-making process. This required several hours of mixing, kneading, rising, punching, kneading, rising, and so on. This was the part of the deal where we kids couldn't jump around because we might interfere with the rising dough, and good things did not happen if one of our slammed doors caved the dough. So after tiptoeing around the house for several hours, the rounded ball was finally ready to be baked. My

Dad would intermittently pace and hover around the oven until the timer buzzed, and then, like clockwork, he would gently pull it out and complain how it wasn't as chewy or puffy as our home-schooling neighbor's. We'd slather butter over every slice and devour it faster than the time it took him to go back down the stairs for more berries to try for fluffier bread.

My long-winded point is that Ruth had a lot of steps to go through in a day. Tedious step upon tedious step followed one another until they eventually led her back to Naomi's doorstep carrying enough sustenance for the two of them: "Ruth also brought out and gave her what she had left over after she had eaten enough." Though seemingly insignificant, this is a defining moment in the story, a definitive change as Ruth moved from dependent to provider. Up to this point we've seen Ruth as committed, loyal, hardworking, and gutsy, but she was very much at the mercy of Boaz and Naomi. We have experienced her as many things but not yet as provider because she hadn't yet had the opportunity.

We've focused on the generosity of Boaz who gave out of his wealth, but now we see Ruth giving out of her poverty! If you can't sense it in my writing, I'm feeling this one. It's hitting me in a very personal place and, yes, this means we all have something to give even if we're broke or broken. This also means we're turning back to 2 Corinthians to read another amazing passage about this truth. You're going to love it.

> We all have something to give even if we're broke or broken.

Mark these statements from 2 Corinthians 8:1-5,9 true or false.

___ **The Macedonian churches gave out of their extreme poverty.**

___ **They gave as much as they were able and no more.**

___ **They saw giving as a painful hardship, but did it anyway (v. 4).**

I'm starting to feel like the person you meet for coffee who does all the talking and won't let you get a word in edgewise. It makes me feel a little better admitting it, but I'm excited about this day in our study because I remember going through painful spells when I was broken, depressed, depleted, and yet it was then—especially then—that God wanted me to give. If you're wondering if I'm talking about money, I'm talking about everything. I'm talking about across-the-board giving: time, resources, advice, teaching, money, comfort, labor ...

Personal Response: All of us are simultaneously rich in some areas and poor in others. So stick with me here on these next two questions and give them some thought:

How can you give out of your wealth?

How can you give out of your poverty?

My respect for Ruth swells every time I read her story. Today she moved into an even higher place of honor in my estimation because of her refusal to wear the mantra of lowly, foreign, bereft servant girl who had nothing to offer. Yes, these labels were true of her experience, but she never wallowed in them and they didn't define her. She had the humility to receive from Boaz's hand and the strength to turn it right around to someone else. Oh, that we might aspire for the humility that can receive another's blessing, mingled with the God-given dignity that always has something to offer.

Lastly, when doing this study with the "nogs," three of the girls had different ideas as to how we should close, so I'm leaving you with three options: (Carrie probably would have had an opinion as well, but she had hosted and cooked and was happy to go with the flow.)

Anadara had a great Personal Response closer: Take time to think of one way you can give to someone today. (I like this because it's specific and requires immediate action.)

Alli thought it would be good to end with a focused time of prayer because we haven't done this in a while.

Lauri admitted to being bugged by specific action questions, so she proposed just ending with "Go and give." Another reason you have to love Lauri.

DAY 05 AN ENCOUNTER
A KINSMAN-REDEEMER

I am overlooking the ocean's sound on the eve of Good Friday. Boats are drifting by; tan reeds wave together in the wind as one collective chorus. I am mindful of the weekend we will mournfully and joyfully observe, slowed down by my surroundings: tepid air, salty water, a few sweet friends, and we're really hoping a fish or two—preferably a large whiting if God answers such prayers.

I can't think it's a coincidence that today of all days on our Western calendar I find myself at the precise bend in our story where a redeemer is to be unveiled. Not *the* Redeemer, whose resurrection we celebrate every year, but a foreshadowing of Him. A human redeemer with the power to restore lives but not souls, whose extraordinary *hesed* could change earthly destinies but not eternal ones. He will bless us and inspire us, but, mostly, he will make us yearn for the ultimate Redeemer, Jesus Christ.

Read Ruth 2:19-23 (I know, you can't believe we're reading five whole verses).

In verse 19, Naomi asked Ruth two questions. What were they?

How did Ruth "answer" Naomi's questions?

I loved a commentator's note about this exchange: "[Naomi] had asked 'where' Ruth had worked; Ruth answers 'with whom' she has worked."[1] Isn't the *who* always so much more significant than the endless *how's, what's,* and *why's* we endlessly fret over? I tend to toil over details, trying to figure how things are going to work out, where help is going to come from. It is then that I am most in need of Jesus. "Be still and know that I am God." Please don't misunderstand me, Naomi's question wasn't bad at all. She even blessed Boaz for taking notice of Ruth. It's just that after Ruth's extraordinary day, she knew the significance wasn't in the *where,* but in the *who*—the person of Boaz.

> Isn't the *who* always so much more significant than the endless *how's, what's, and why's* we endlessly fret over?

Naomi went on to bless this man while also saying, "He has not stopped showing his kindness to the living and the dead." One important note is that the "He" to whom Naomi referred is a bit unclear, whether it is the Lord or Boaz. Most scholars agree that she referred to Yahweh; but either way, for our purposes, we can credit God as ultimately showing her kindness, whether directly or through Boaz.

But there's more to this beautiful line. The most exact rendering is: "Who has not abandoned his kindness [hesed] toward the living and the dead."[2] If indeed Naomi is referring to God here, how different this comment is to some of her earlier ones.

> **Personal Take: Read Ruth 1:20-21. How has Naomi's attitude to God drastically changed, and why do you suppose? (Turn back to day I, session 2 if you need to refresh your memory.)**

Remember that *hesed* is one of the most powerful phrases of covenant love and loyalty in the Hebrew language *(kindness* just doesn't do the meaning justice). How interesting that only recently had Naomi charged God as the One who brought her misfortune and bitterness, but now she sees that … wait a minute … He has not abandoned her after all.

I have a worn King James Bible that is marked to bits from my high school and college years. I dealt with a good bit of anxiety and depression growing up, so my Bible is disproportionately highlighted in certain places, not the least of which is in the psalms. When I read about Naomi's sudden change of heart, my mind immediately flashed back to that old Bible and a specific underlined verse that administered much comfort to my frightened soul.

Psalm 31:22
In my alarm I said, "I am cut off from your sight!" Yet you heard my cry for mercy when I called to you for help.

> **Read Psalm 31:22 in the margin or from your favorite translation.**

The King James Version says "in my haste," and I imagine Naomi and the rest of us can relate to this. How often have our difficult circumstances propelled us to determine in alarm or haste that God has abandoned us? The psalmist said that in his haste he jumped to this conclusion, but later realized that, no, God had heard his cry for mercy after all. In our reading today we see Naomi make this similar shift.

SESSION 03 AN ENCOUNTER

Personal Response: Write about a time you prematurely decided God had abandoned you or was against you. How did your perspective change? Or if you're there right now, write about it.

Whom did Naomi specifically reveal Boaz to be in verse 20?

It's interesting that up to this point Naomi knew she had a kinsman-redeemer named Boaz but had no idea Ruth knew him; Ruth knew Boaz but didn't know he was a kinsman-redeemer. Suddenly these two pieces of information collided to potentially change the course of history. Not only was Boaz an extraordinarily helpful and kind man, he was a close relative of Naomi's (2:1), a kinsman-redeemer or a "goel" in the Hebrew. Much like *hesed, goel* is another very important Hebrew word in the Book of Ruth that needs to be further defined. (Also note that I will use it interchangeably with the term *kinsman-redeemer.*)

"Goel was a term from the realm of Israelite family law. It describes not a precise kinship relationship but the near relatives to whom both law and custom gave certain duties toward the clan."[3]

"As a kinship term it denotes the near relative who is responsible for the economic well-being of a relative, and he comes into play especially when the relative is in distress and cannot get himself/herself out of the crisis. … The custom of redemption was designed to maintain the wholeness and health of family relationships, even after the person has died."[4]

You can read about the traditional role of a kinsman-redeemer in Leviticus 25:25-30. What is the nearest relative (kinsman-redeemer/goel) able to do?

A kinsman-redeemer's role has several additional aspects:
1. To ensure that the hereditary property of the clan never passes out of the clan (Lev. 25:25-30).

2. To maintain the freedom of the individuals within the clan by buying back those who have sold themselves into slavery because of poverty (Lev. 25:47-55).
3. To track down and execute murderers of near relatives (Num. 35:12,19-27).
4. To receive restitution money on behalf of a deceased victim of a crime (Num. 5:8).
5. To ensure that justice is served in a lawsuit involving a relative (Job 19:25; Ps. 119:154; Jer. 50:34).[5]

May our hearts grow with deeper appreciation for our one true Redeemer, Jesus, the most unique of all.

One reason I want you to firmly understand the *goel* in Scripture is because it so beautifully helps us further understand not just Boaz, but how Jesus has uniquely redeemed us. As we become further enamored with Boaz, so our hearts will grow with deeper appreciation for our one true Redeemer, Jesus, the most unique of all.

In closing, read Galatians 3:13-15; 4:3-7.

Personal Response: As a result of studying the Old Testament law of redemption, in what new way(s) do you understand Jesus' redemption of you?

No doubt we've covered a lot of ground, though perhaps not as wide as deep. Digging into Old Testament law, peeking into Revelation, reading about people with names like Mephibosheth, enduring a study on humility, committing to give more, and learning about wheat berries (Mike would be so proud), are not for the timid. I'm really honored that you'd journey with me here. So my deepest thanks for walking with me to the halfway point. Go celebrate with some type of sugary complex-carbohydrate (donut with sprinkles) and some coffee. And sit with someone who doesn't talk so much …

Redeeming Love

Sarah Hart & Kelly Minter
See the story behind the song at www.livingroomseries.com.

What binds a life to another one
And frees our every inhibition
What moves the heart from despairing
To the hope that all is forgiven

Who knows the sorrows we've hidden away
And makes Himself at home among us
Who makes all things bright and beautiful
From our brokenness

Chorus
Redeemer, ever nearer
To the broken hearted
Strong Savior, Tender Healer
Cover us in Your redeeming love

How strong the arms that surround us,
Oh, how sweet the voice that sings our name
Beside this merciful river You cleanse
Our inmost shame

Chorus

Bridge
Love that reaches to the farthest ones
Love that makes us daughters and sons
Love that sweeps us underneath its wings
Love that gives us back a song to sing

Kelly Minter & Sarah Hart. Mintyfresh Music (ASCAP). Sarah Hart (administered by
Spiritandsongcom and EMI-CMG)/River Oaks Music (administered by EMI-CMG)/BMI.

To purchase this song or CD go to
www.LifeWay.com/livingroomseries.

GRILLED CHICKEN SALAD WITH STRAWBERRIES

SERVES 6

I make this all the time. Once you get it down, you'll be looking for whole chickens at every turn. You'll never want to do grocery store rotisserie again. I served it the first night of our study.

1 3-4 lb. whole chicken
2 tablespoons olive oil
1 large head red leaf lettuce
6 oz. Feta cheese
olive oil
salt and pepper to taste

1 can of soft drink
spice rub (Greek or Cajun)
1 cup sliced strawberries
1½ cups shelled walnuts
balsamic vinegar

Directions for chicken: Rinse chicken with cold water inside and out. Pat dry with paper towels. Rub olive oil on the outside of the bird and your favorite seasoning on the inside (such as Cavender's or Cajun seasoning mix).

If you have a vertical chicken roaster, pour half of the soft drink into its built-in cylinder and place the bird upright on the cylinder. OR, remove the whole top of the soft drink with a can opener. Pour out half. Add some seasoning mix to the remaining liquid. Set the bird upright on top of the can (it should go about halfway into the cavity). Then place the chicken on the can upright on your grill. I preheat the grill for several minutes then leave one side up on a higher heat setting while placing the chicken on the other side and turning the flame down to a medium- to medium-low setting. Let the chicken slowly cook on the grill for about 45 minutes and then check the temperature with a meat thermometer. Bird is done when it is 160° in the breast area and 180° in the thigh area. Slice chicken after letting it cool.

Directions for salad: Pre-heat oven to 350° for walnuts. Place walnuts on a cookie sheet and cook until toasted. Wash red leaf lettuce and tear into bite-sized pieces, using a salad spinner if you have one. Place prepared lettuce in salad bowl. Add sliced strawberries, toasted walnuts, feta cheese, and sliced chicken. Add olive oil and balsamic vinegar to taste and toss.

BANOFFI PIE
PRE-HEAT OVEN TO 400° SERVES 6-8

If you try only one recipe, this is the one! I ate this at the Hungry Monk Restaurant in England where it was invented.

1½ cups graham cracker crumbs
10 tablespoons butter, melted
2 14-oz. cans sweetened condensed milk
3 large bananas
1½ cups heavy whipping cream
⅓ cup confectioners' sugar
1 teaspoon vanilla
½ teaspoon powdered instant coffee
freshly ground coffee or chocolate shavings

Directions
Mix graham cracker crumbs with melted butter and press mixture into 9" pie plate. Bake for 5 to 8 minutes. Allow to cool.

Immerse the unopened cans of sweetened uncondensed milk in a deep pan of boiling water. Cover and boil for 3 hours, making sure the cans remain covered with water. (Add water as needed.) Remove the cans from the water; allow to cool completely before opening.

Whip the cream with the sugar, vanilla, and instant coffee until thick and smooth. Spread ⅓ of the toffee over the base of the crust. Slice the bananas and lay them on the toffee. Spoon another ⅓ of toffee over the bananas. Layer more bananas and more toffee. Finally, spoon or pipe on the cream and lightly sprinkle with the freshly ground coffee or chocolate shavings.

Note: Boiling milk in the can carries some risk. You can find alternate cooking methods at *www.verybestbaking.com/recipes* or other Web sites.

I AM FALLING IN LOVE WITH RUTH AND HER STORY . . .

AND AM JUST BEGINNING TO UNDERSTAND WHY I HAVE BEEN SO THOROUGHLY CAPTURED. OF COURSE THERE ARE THE OBVIOUS PULLS OF A BURGEONING ROMANCE AND THE GRABBING STORY LINE OF TWO WOMEN WHO HAVE WALKED THROUGH TRAGEDY AND ARE STILL, WELL, WALKING . . . THERE ARE THE HONEST HAPPENINGS, LIKE NAOMI'S BITTERNESS ERUPTING ALL OVER GOD WHEN SOMEONE ASKED THE SIMPLEST OF QUESTIONS: "IS THIS REALLY NAOMI?" THERE'S A LOT TO BE ENVELOPED BY, THOUGH FOR ME ONE CONSISTENT THREAD HAS KNIT ITS WAY INTO MY SOUL, NOT LETTING ME OFF ITS SPOOL: RUTH'S ABANDONMENT TO LIVING ON THE EXTREME EDGE OF HER FAITH. RUTH'S DECISIONS HAVE NOT BEEN MADE OUT OF SELFISH AMBITION OR EVEN NORMAL REASON BUT OUT OF A PURSUIT OF GOD THAT IS ANYTHING BUT ORDINARY. FOR ME, THERE HAS BEEN NO SKIRTING THIS.

Her story and choices light up against the status quo. Where Orpah turned around, Ruth kept going. Where Naomi blamed God for her loss, Ruth declared Him her Lord. I don't think Orpah or Naomi were "bad" characters, just normal ones. Mostly they did what any one of us would do given similar circumstances. But normal is a very insidious trap to fall into when you're talking about having the Spirit of God living inside you. I'm afraid it's where I too often reside, though I'm more and more discontented there. Especially after I've ventured out by the leading of the Holy Spirit, and I do the unconventional or even the "foolish" and experience the invigorating excitement of being about the things Christ is passionate about; and I remember that, yes, this is where I want to live.

I sat outside with some friends last night, well after the sun had set, pondering life over linguini tossed in olive oil with fresh garlic, basil, black olives, feta, and tomatoes, and there you go (see p. 62 for the recipe). We were surrounded by flickering tiki torches, like a little jungle party, that did a remarkable job of warding off the mosquitoes but were worthless when it came to the slugs. I found one on my plate. I'm glad we weren't having penne or ziti, as this could have gotten sorely confusing in the dark.

We mused about something I promise I don't excessively chew on—singleness. But occasionally it just has to be addressed. Like when your younger siblings are getting married and having children, or someone you know is planning her third wedding, or the grass needs cutting. I don't even remember what got us on to this, but when I asked one of my beautiful, single friends if she felt she would ever get married, she looked off with glinty eyes, "I don't let myself go there." The problem was that our conversation was beginning to take her there and her emotions caught her off guard. After my friend's honest statement, I started wondering how many amazing women—whether it's about singleness, childlessness, or other unfulfilled dreams—are doing life but don't ever let themselves "go there."

Mostly I think we stay away because we're afraid of what we might discover: We don't want to hurt or ache. We're fearful of finding out who God really is in relation to our deepest longings. Will He withhold from us? Will we be betrayed? abandoned?

And so we don't venture to those places, closing them off with fortified walls because it's not safe to long there. I really should have waited at least until this morning before blurting, "You must go there!" but I couldn't restrain myself, exhorting her to go there with God—that she could trust Him. This was earnest encouragement. Solid, friendship advice. Well-meaning. My timing could have been better.

What is simultaneously inspiring and convicting this week is that Ruth is about to "go there." Without prematurely unveiling the details, Ruth is on the brink of heading to a threshing floor under the canopy of night, alone. Because, let's face it, some places we can only go with God by ourselves—there's just no way to take anyone with us. And once Ruth gets to the threshing floor there will be no guarantees. She has been promised nothing. Her venture was not a demand on God, "If I take the risk of going there, then You must do …" It was simply a walk of faith, a humble obedience with no strings attached. And this is the way we must approach our own threshing floors. Without demands. Sometimes in the dark. Alone. But with the expectation that God will always be found faithful and good.

I hope this primes your heart for the week ahead. It is perhaps our most personal week this far, so if you're inclined to give tidy, Christian answers with half your heart walled off (a penchant for all of us), my prayer is that you would pry back those gates—even if it means a mini-Naomi tantrum. (It's possible that God is more inclined to tend to our outbursts than our detached silence.) Because there are great rewards at the threshing floor—not rewards we necessarily get to handpick—but ones God chooses for us that are beyond our imagination. The passage is worth whatever we are protecting ourselves from, this I am sure. With trepidation, with fear, with teary eyes, however you must go … go there. We can't afford not to.

DAY 01 A PROPOSAL
A MOTHER-IN-LAW'S REQUEST

I hope you're ready for this week because things are about to really heat up between Ruth and Boaz. Yes, I know this is a Bible study, but I'm talking about *that* kind of hot. The other day I picked up a really old commentary on the Book of Ruth and had to smile because the author completely skipped over the passage we're about to read—not glossed or skimmed but hopped it like a fence. Perhaps this commentary was written during a time when it wasn't acceptable to reference things sexual or romantic, but since it's, well, in the Bible, I feel pretty good about going there.

But right before we take the plunge, I want us to note that a certain amount of time has passed since we closed last week with Naomi and Ruth recognizing Boaz as their kinsman-redeemer. We didn't get a chance to focus on the closing verse of chapter 2, but I want you to revisit it because it speaks to this time lapse, which is important.

Take time to read all of Ruth 2. How long did Ruth glean in Boaz's field (v. 23)?

With whom did she live during that time?

Ruth worked and stayed with Naomi through the barley and wheat harvest, which would have been from late April to early June. It's important to note that some time passed between chapters 2 and 3. I didn't want you to think that once Naomi and Ruth recognized Boaz as their *goel* things turned around right there on the spot. I can relate to this, because discovering a solution (in their case, Boaz), doesn't always mean I don't have to wait for it. I can think of a few times when I was given a promise or sensed God bringing a change, but I had to be patient for its fulfillment. With just this little bit of information we're ready to begin chapter 3.

Read Ruth 3:1-6 and write down a few things that surprise you about these verses.

Discovering a solution doesn't always mean we don't have to wait for it.

Naomi's significant change of heart toward Ruth's well-being really hits me. It's not like she didn't care before; she just didn't want to deal with her. But now we find her quite concerned with finding Ruth a husband. Unlike verses 8-9, where Naomi was shooing Ruth back to the Moabites and asking God to bring her a husband, here I get the impression that Naomi had really come to love Ruth as one of her own and was now embracing the task herself.

By what new title did Naomi address Ruth in 3:1, and how does this speak to her change of heart?

This is the second time we've seen Naomi refer to Boaz as a kinsman-redeemer of "ours" (Ruth 2:20; 3:2). Naomi now recognized Ruth as family. There's no question that Ruth's loyal and relentless love toward Naomi have sweetened her bitterness and quelled her hopelessness. Ruth has imperceptibly rooted her way right into Naomi's heart before Naomi could do a thing about it. This should give us hope for even the hardest of people we've been called to love.

Personal Response: Is someone in your life difficult to love?

Naomi and Ruth's relationship will continue to offer us hope for our own ailing relationships. But for now, we're going to move on to the really spicy stuff 'cause who can't appreciate someone else's drama on occasion? Is this not why we go to the movies? Especially when it comes to romance, mothers-in-law getting involved, and men who are slow to the party. I find this all quite entertaining, especially when Naomi "innocently" says, "Is not Boaz ... a kinsman of ours?" As if to say, "Why ever haven't I thought of this before?" Who knows how long Naomi had this particular scheme brewing, but we give her kudos for creativity, innovation, and feigning like this was the first time the concept had crossed her mind.

List Naomi's instructions to Ruth in the order they were given.

Let's tackle a few of these because some of them definitely need further explanation. First, washing and perfuming herself and putting on certain clothes were meant to accomplish everything you'd think. The intent was for Ruth to be her most attractive and presentable (not seductive but attractive). The common translation of Ruth wearing her "best clothes" is not a good rendering, but we're going to save this discussion for tomorrow. It requires a day all its own.

The threshing floor is an interesting place for Naomi to have sent Ruth, especially under the cover of dark. This was not like sending her to church for single's pizza night. In ancient Israel, especially during winnowing season, the threshing floor was often linked with sexual activity. Since men would sleep next to their piles of grain, prostitutes knew this to be a place where they could offer their services, making it a compromising and suggestive environment.

In addition to the precarious nature of the time and place—not to mention that Ruth was smelling and looking like a little Moabite rose— Naomi told Ruth to not go over to Boaz until after he had something to eat and drink. More than likely this drink was alcoholic and, though not excessive, would have lowered his guard a bit. Add to all of these elements Naomi's instruction for Ruth to wait until Boaz had fallen asleep to uncover his feet and lie down next to him, and we have a really risky—or risqué—situation.

The idea of uncovering Boaz's feet is another difficult picture for us modern-day readers to understand. Scholars have mused about it meaning everything from uncovering sexual organs, to nakedness, to his actual feet. Because many scholars support it meaning his feet and there is no supporting context for it to concretely mean anything other than that, we're going to go with this assumption. Nonetheless, lying down at his uncovered feet was still a vulnerable position for Ruth.

> **How many of Naomi's instructions did Ruth carry out (v. 6)?**
>
> **After completing this list, what was Ruth to wait for (v. 4)?**
>
> **Personal Response: Describe a time when you'd done everything you could do and then had to wait for someone else's response.**

My personal opinion is that Naomi was an honorable woman who didn't intend to promote promiscuous behavior between Ruth and Boaz. I believe her intentions were born out of a desire to see someone love and care for Ruth. However, I think in her zeal to accomplish something very good she compromised Ruth and Boaz by putting them in a dangerous situation. Again, this is just my personal take. I would love to know how you've assimilated all these details. Perhaps I tend to see it this way because on occasion when I've wanted something inherently good I went about accomplishing it in a manner that was not nearly as pure.

> **For Discussion: Write down your thoughts about Naomi's plan. Do you think it was good, shrewd, risqué, brilliant? I don't believe there's a right or wrong answer, but give it some thought.**

One of the most remarkable and mysterious parts of life is how our frail and human plans somehow fit into God's master plan.

No matter how we deem Naomi's plot, one of the most remarkable and mysterious parts of life is how our frail and human plans somehow fit into God's master plan. The wisdom of Scripture sums this up best:

> **Next to each verse write a quick description of how God ultimately controls our plans.**
>
> **Proverbs 20:24**
>
> **Proverbs 16:1**
>
> **Proverbs 21:30-31**
>
> **Jeremiah 10:23**

Be blessed today that God's supremacy and providence reign over all our plans, for He directs our steps.

DAY 02 A PROPOSAL
A NEW DAY

Today is deeply personal as we look at the risk and symbolism involved in Ruth's visiting the threshing floor in the dead of night. Yesterday we looked at the more technical side, discovering what some of the foreign practices meant in their culture. But today I am moved by the courage and heart that propelled Ruth, especially since I as a single woman like to take things slowly when it comes to dating. And when I say slowly, I mean for the first four months I might just want to meet for coffee. That's before moving onto something far more serious, like say, brunch. I had a very wonderful guy recently lay down the law, "Look, enough coffee. I'm picking you up for breakfast. We will eat toast and have granola and eggs. I will order us the bread basket." In my parallel universe this felt like breakneck speed, but when I read about Ruth and the whole threshing floor ordeal, I realized that committing to French toast isn't nearly as threatening as I once thought.

Personal Take: Look at Ruth 1:3-5. How might these past events have added to Ruth's difficulty of carrying out Naomi's plan?

Scripture doesn't reveal the inner conversation Ruth had as she discreetly walked to the threshing floor, but as women we may have a reasonable idea of how her heart was fluttering, what fears she wrestled, how often she thought about darting back to Naomi's, wondering whether she had misread Boaz's cues of kindness as meaning something they did not. Would her heart be broken again? Would Boaz reject her? And in the slim chance he wanted her, could she risk the possibility of tragedy striking twice? I imagine that at every step the list of reasons for turning around mounted, though perhaps the same resolve that got her to Bethlehem also carried her to the threshing floor that night. I can only hope for such courage.

Personal Response: Describe a time when your obedience to God felt like a risk. What did you learn in the process?

Simla: an outer garment that covered virtually the entire body except the head

Yesterday I told you we'd further explore the clothing Ruth wore to meet Boaz, per Naomi's instruction. You'll remember that the translation "put on your best clothes" is not accurate according to the original language. The Hebrew word used to describe what Ruth wore was a fairly generic term, *simla*. It normally referred to an outer garment that covered virtually the entire body except the head. Some commentators believe that Ruth dressed as a bride based on other extrabiblical passages that follow a similar pattern, but it's safe to say we don't know exactly what she was wearing. It's just not explicitly clear. What we do know, however, is that Ruth—whatever she had on—was dressed for a new day.

Scholar Daniel I. Block has some fascinating insight: "It appears that Naomi is hereby advising Ruth to end her period of mourning over her widowhood and get on with normal life. ... It may well be that until this time Ruth had always worn the garments of widowhood, even when she was working out in the field. Perhaps this was the reason for Boaz's inertia. As an upright man, he would not violate a woman's right to grieve the loss of her husband nor impose himself upon her until she was ready. We know too little about how long widows would customarily wear their mourning clothes, but it may be that Naomi is now telling Ruth the time has come to doff her 'garments of widowhood.' "[1]

This last line slays me. Though many of us have not experienced the unspeakable and incomprehensible tragedy of losing a spouse or someone we loved deeply, we have known a time when God asked us to take off our clothes of mourning, clinging, grasping, wishing, hoping, striving, even praying for something ... and move forward. I specifically remember a moment when God made this exact request of me. I had been clinging to the past, hanging on to the last ragged edges of something He had worked hard to move me on from. Goodness, *I* had worked hard to move on from it. But one night I read a convicting passage in Scripture that helped move me forward.

The story is found in 1 Samuel 15–16 and gives the details of the fall of King Saul. The very abridged version is this: Samuel had anointed Saul king over Israel so he had a personal interest in him and his success. Tragically, Saul proved to be a disobedient king, causing God to take the kingdom from his hands. Saul's disobedience and the tearing away of the kingdom left Samuel in mourning for many years (15:35). But after all this mourning, the Lord had a specific question for Samuel.

Read 1 Samuel 16:1. What was the question?

What did God then ask Samuel to do?

I remember reading this story when the Lord asked me how long I was going to mourn for the old because, indeed, He had something new for me ahead. It was time for me to move forward—without my mourning clothes. Here's the deal: When we're wrapped in garments of mourning, we're unavailable for whatever else God has for us. In a sense, we take ourselves out of the game. Though we can't be certain what Ruth had on, we know her new dress signaled a change, a readiness, an availability to Boaz and to God for the possibility of something new.

Please know that if you have walked Ruth's exact journey of a dire loss, I am not at all presuming on your grieving process. My simple hope is when God has held us, healed us, and lifted our heads, that we'd be ready to move forward with Him; and though our hearts may always ache, we won't stay in our mourning clothes forever.

Isaiah 54 is an inspiring passage about God's love and faithfulness to the Israelites. It almost makes me wonder if the author had Ruth in mind for a moment when writing. Read verses 1-5.

According to verse 4, what will be remembered no more?

Verse 4 doesn't say we won't remember our "widowhood," but the reproach of it. God may not remove the memory, but He's able to take the sting out of it as He was on the brink of doing for Ruth. There are things that I fully recall from my past that don't hurt like they used to, and I praise God for His healing.

Do you sense that God is asking you to throw off some weighty garments? Unforgiveness, bitterness, anger, discontentment, jealousy, mourning, or anything else that might be keeping you in a stagnant place? While walking on the beach the other day, a tiny little boy bounded by me, clothed only by the ocean's breeze, reminding me of such weightlessness—on a spiritual plane, but of course.

> When we're wrapped in garments of mourning, we're unavailable for whatever else God has for us.

If you sense God's nudging, describe your situation and take a moment to prayerfully hand those worn clothes over to Him. (Don't rush this if God is speaking. Take the time to address it.)

I want to leave you with one of my favorite passages in the entire Bible. I know I say this a lot, but I have different favorites for different things. It's a little like jeans: I've got my favorite flip-flop jeans, working, performing, laying-around-in pairs. I even have my favorite Southern Baptist jeans which, I know, sound like the scariest things ever; but they're the dressier ones I can just barely get away with speaking in on occasion. But I digress.

Flip back a few chapters and read Isaiah 43:18-19.

Fill in the blank: "Forget the former things; do not _____ on the past."

There's something about where our minds choose to dwell that can keep us in an old place even when God is doing a new thing—when He's holding out a new dress for us. Isaiah 52:1 says, "Awake, awake, O Zion, clothe yourself with strength. Put on your garments of splendor, O Jerusalem, the holy city." This is an Old Testament plea to the Israelites, but I dare say that the One who has given us new life—Jesus Christ—is calling us to the same awakening, the same new set of clothes. Do not dwell on the past! Yes, we all have our Moab stories, our past losses, aches, and stains; but let us not cling to our old clothes in a new life.

Read Ephesians 4:22-24. How can you specifically put these verses into practice?

Take off the old, put on the new; take the risk of being available.

Take off the old, put on the new; take the risk of being available. You may not be up for a midnight visit to the threshing floor, but, hey, baby steps and French toast is what I say. "Therefore, if anyone is in Christ, he is a new creation; the old has past, the new has come!" (2 Cor. 5:17).

DAY 03 A PROPOSAL
LAY DOWN

Nothing's quite so vulnerable as the first time you lay out your feelings for someone in a relationship. The anxiety of filleting yourself in front of the only person in the world whose feelings for you matter at the moment has rendered the brave fluttering and the eloquent tongue-tied. Such heart exposure wouldn't be so bad if only we could be convinced of what would greet us on the other side. Will our undying love be gloriously requited, or will we be met with confusion, rejection, or worse yet, the "let's be friends" conversation? After a recent first date, one of my best friends got the "I don't think I should be dating anyone right now" e-mail. To which I really, really wanted her to write something back like, "Well, then, maybe you should stop asking women out on dates!" And this was my super nice version. It just wouldn't be right to print the other one in a Bible study.

If proclaiming love for another person can be risky, Ruth's current situation is in a league all its own. She loved and lost before, was a lowly foreigner seeking a wealthy Israelite, was a woman proposing to a man (which was countercultural at best), and she was in a place she hadn't been invited. In poker terms I think this would be considered "all in."

I'm excited for you to read about the details in Ruth 3:5-9.

What kind of a mood was Boaz in after eating and drinking?

disgruntled   melancholy and pensive

ecstatic   in good spirits

How did Boaz come to find someone at his feet?

Daniel I. Block again has interesting insight, "Given the spiritual climate in the period of the judges, an average Israelite might have welcomed the night visit of a woman, interpreting her presence as an offer of sexual favors, but not so Boaz."[2] Remember that the story of Ruth took

> Nothing's quite so vulnerable as the first time you lay out your feelings for someone in a relationship.

Philippians 2:15
So that you may become blameless and pure, children of God without fault in a crooked and depraved generation, in which you shine like stars in the universe.

place during the rule of the Judges, which were difficult and dark days. Here we see a real moral uprightness in Boaz that pops against the backdrop of a time when most did whatever they "saw fit" in their own eyes. This should encourage us to hold fast to the beliefs and morals the Scriptures treasure even when society mocks. (See Phil. 2:15.)

I'm sure you noticed the additional step Ruth added to Naomi's list of instructions. Describe how Ruth veered from Naomi's plan.

Read Ezekiel 16:8 to further understand the action of a man spreading his skirt over a woman. Between this verse and Ruth 3:9, what do you think Ruth was asking of Boaz?

In case anyone is confused by the terminology of men wearing skirts and spreading them over women, let me plainly say that Ruth was asking Boaz to marry her.

Personal Take: Why do you think Ruth jumped in with a marriage proposal instead of waiting on Boaz like Naomi instructed? Give it some thought before writing your answer here.

After following almost all of Naomi's instructions flawlessly, she wildly veered from them at the end. Instead of waiting for Boaz's instructions (3:4), she whipped out a marriage proposal. Oh my. I love Ruth so much I can hardly stand it. She was brave, bold, humble, and thoroughly shocking! And let me tuck in here that it was not out of Ruth's single desperation or reckless nervousness that she made this request. Many scholars suggest that Ruth was selflessly thinking of Naomi when she asked Boaz to marry her, knowing that his redemption of her would also ensure Naomi's future security. Her *hesed* here is extraordinary.

Technically, the word *skirt* or *garment* can be translated more precisely as *wings*. More accurately it might read, *Spread your wings over your handmaid*. I love the use of the word *wings* here because it's reminiscent of an earlier conversation Ruth and Boaz had.

Look back at Ruth 2:12, and write out Boaz's prayer for Ruth.

This is so amazing because essentially Ruth was asking Boaz to be the answer to his own prayer! Similarly, I believe this happened when Naomi prayed that Ruth would find a husband, only to later find out God would answer her prayer for Ruth by raising Naomi up to help accomplish the very thing she prayed for (1:9).

There's something really convicting hiding in these passages. Both Naomi and Boaz spoke prayers over Ruth that they ended up fulfilling. We should never cease praying or undermine its unparalleled power, and yet sometimes God calls us to add some action to our prayers. We can get into the habit of uttering half-hearted "God bless blah, blah, blah," "God help so and so," "Lord, be with this or that person," when really God is saying back to us something to the effect of, "I will as soon as you get in there!" Both Naomi and Boaz were the answers to their own prayers for Ruth's life. What a remarkable thought!

> Sometimes God calls us to add some action to our prayers.

Personal Response: Describe something you've prayed a lot about but haven't been very active in. What can you do to change this?

Look back at Ruth 3:7 and fill in the blank: "Ruth approached quietly, uncovered his feet and _____ _____."

All of Ruth's anxieties, apprehensions, fears, wonderings, and emotions culminate with these two words. She had lost her husband, left her family, moved to a foreign country, inserted herself in the fields, submitted to her mother in-law, journeyed to the threshing floor, and now, after all this time, she must simply lie down. She had cast her life, her future, even the legacy of her deceased husband, at the feet of Boaz; there was nothing to do now but rest and wait.

This place of surrender is the most freeing of places to be and the hardest to get to. Some of us have been working, toiling, and struggling—we've done all we can do and now it's time to cease striving and lie down at the feet of Jesus. I'm not sure what plagues you, what you're carrying, or what fears loom in your life. But I want you to picture leaving those things behind, as if you were Ruth standing at the edge of the threshing floor, knowing that she couldn't bring anything with her—only herself. Here are a few verses that will help you move across your own threshing floor to the feet of Christ so you can freely lie down.

Read each verse slowly and thoughtfully as you envision getting to that place of rest. I've left room for you to jot notes by the verses that are most meaningful to you.

Proverbs 3:5-6

Matthew 10:39

Matthew 11:28-30

Romans 12:1-2

I wish I could individually address you at this moment, as I'm not sure there is any more important move in our life with Christ than our total surrender to Him. Yes, this can be scary. Yes, it can be costly. But as we'll soon see in Ruth's story, the earthly and eternal blessings of submission to Jesus are unparalleled. What He can do with a willing life surrendered at His feet is more than we can comprehend. I just know I don't want to miss it for whatever I'm clutching in my hands.

What Christ can do with a willing life surrendered at His feet is more than we can comprehend.

Personal Response:

What keeps you from resting under your Redeemer's wings?

Write your prayer of surrender here:

I LAY DOWN

Sarah Hart & Kelly Minter
See the story behind the song at www.livingroomseries.com.

I have journeyed so far
I'm getting tired of being strong
I am losing heart
I'm ready to live where I belong
Oh, where could I go
But to the heart that calls me home

Chorus
I lay down at your feet
And your mercy covers me
I am bound to be free
In the shelter of your wings
I lay down

I have walked afraid
Stumbled through darkness by myself
Just to see your face
To behold you and no one else
Oh, where could I go
But to the heart that knows my own

Chorus

Bridge
You are my hope, You are my peace
You have always been and will always be
For I once was lost and now I've been found
I lay down, I lay down

Kelly Minter & Sarah Hart. *Spiritandsong.com* Publishing/River Oaks
Music Co. (BMI) (Admin. By EMI CMG Publishing). Mintyfresh Music (ASCAP)

DAY 04 A PROPOSAL
A CLOSER RELATIVE

Ruth was a seamless blend of confidence and humility, strength and deference, knowing what she wanted but knowing her place.

I guess we really shouldn't be surprised by now, but is anyone just a little astounded by Ruth's sheer amazing-ness? (My vocabulary fails me.) Here's what I am loving about her: She was a seamless blend of confidence and humility, strength and deference, knowing what she wanted but knowing her place. It's hard to get this right without coming off as brash and arrogant or pitiful and self-deprecating. I believe it was Ruth's total abandonment and obedience to God that allowed her to strike this remarkable balance. "Unless God's inspiration had been in Ruth, she would not have said what she said or done what she did."[3] I am inclined to want to emulate her bravery and determination, and yet I am reminded that it was the breath of God that carried her to such heights. Her story reminds me of Psalm 18:35, which says that God stoops down to make us great. Yes, this is about Ruth, but so much more about our God.

I hope you're up for a little twist today. After all, things are beginning to go almost too well, and this usually doesn't make for the most interesting of reads. Not that Scripture is here for our entertainment, but I'm all for grabbing the popcorn when the opportunity arises.

Read Ruth 3:10-13.

Personal Take: What do you think Boaz meant when he said that Ruth's kindness (hesed) was greater than what she had shown earlier? (Look back at 2:11 to be reminded of her earlier hesed.)

Fill in the blank: "All my fellow townsmen know that you are a woman of _____ _____."

I would love better skin—smaller pores and fewer speckles, to be exact. I wish my features were a bit more angular and less rounded. I would like more melatonin, less shocking whiteness. But if I could have any adjustment to my spiritual self, I would say more noble character. Pluck, prod, dermabrase, Lord, do what You need to do—I want to be one of those women who is known for her character. I didn't know this prior to studying the Book of Ruth, but the Hebrew Bible places Proverbs right before Ruth, which means the description of the Proverbs 31 woman leads straight into Ruth's story. (Those of us who tend to have a penchant toward theological nerdiness will find this thrilling.)

Read Proverbs 31:10-31, and don't get all stressed out about how insanely perfect this woman seems and how we all feel like sloths compared to her. Not the point of this passage, I promise. Instead, study her character. Look for the areas you'd like God to bolster in your life. She's inspiring, if you'll let her be. Trust me, God can speak through such irritating perfection.

Personal Response:
List the things that remind you of Ruth.

What things do you admire about her that you'd like to see strengthened in your own life?

Verse 31 says this woman will be praised where?

Keeping this detail in mind, turn back to Ruth 3:11. Most translations say the "people in the city" or "fellow townsmen" knew Ruth was a woman of noble character, but the actual translation is, "all the gate of my people." It essentially means the same thing as all the people, but when the word "gate" is not included, we miss the significance. Iain Duguid explains it this way, "The idiom is usually lost in translation, but what we see in Ruth [3:11] is precisely a 'Proverbs 31' woman in the flesh; her deeds have indeed been praised in the city gates!"[4]

> **Ruth 3:11**
> My daughter, don't be afraid. I will do for you all you ask. All my fellow townsmen know that you are a woman of noble character.

We talked a little bit about this at the top of week 3, but I am even further taken with the notion that Ruth's character has been the fire spreading her fame. It's not who she aligned herself with, who she manipulated, her wealth, her beauty, her publicist; it's not about her heritage, her singing talent, or athletic prowess. It's about the *hesed* she had shown Naomi and Yahweh. It's about her character. And much like the woman in Proverbs 31:31, she was being rewarded and esteemed at the "city gate."

Personal Response: How does the celebration of Ruth's character encourage you to be faithful in the quiet and small, everyday things? (Matt. 6:18b and Luke 16:10 also speak of this principle.)

OK, you've been so patient, dutifully reading about character and noble women and answering questions; but I know what you're thinking: Get on with it already! Who's this nearer kinsman redeemer? We want Boaz! And I am wholeheartedly behind you, so let's look into this.

The existence of a nearer kinsman redeemer may explain why Boaz didn't propose to Ruth earlier and why the poor thing had to prostrate herself on the threshing floor asking for an engagement. We can't be sure, but we do know this really throws a wrench in our love story. If this unnamed relative should choose to redeem her, Boaz would have to step aside. And what's more, after this staggering information, Boaz told Ruth to essentially sleep tight. I doubt that Ruth slept for two seconds that night. I would have laid there bug-eyed, staring up at the night sky, wondering what I had gotten myself into—if Naomi's whole scheme was God-inspired or if she was perfectly crazy.

What did Boaz promise to do if the nearer relative chose not to redeem Ruth?

For Discussion: Use the room in the margin to describe both the relief and tension Ruth must have felt after hearing Boaz's favorable response to her request, mixed with the news that someone else might redeem her. Really put yourself in her place as you describe your thoughts.

If Ruth slept at all that night, she must have slipped imperceptibly from reality, for who could possibly tell the difference between this and a dream? A Moabitess, a widow, poor and with no standing, lay at the feet of a noble and powerful man who this time didn't just invite her for lunch or leave extra sheaves but wanted her to be his wife. Ruth's dreams and reality began to lap into each other like colliding waves: The unthinkable had happened—Boaz wanted to redeem her. Whether or not he could is a different story. But for the first time since arriving in Bethlehem, Ruth went to sleep knowing he wanted to.

DAY 05 A PROPOSAL
A GIFT TO GIVE

Something about yesterday's setting reminds me of another critical night in Scripture when a Redeemer and those waiting to be redeemed had to endure unsettling darkness for morning's answer. It was at Gethsemane when Jesus asked His disciples to keep watch during the midnight hours preceding His arrest. But their willing spirits couldn't prop their heavy eyelids, and they slept as their Redeemer's life hung in the balance. At this point in our study, the fate of Ruth's redeemer is in question as well. Yes, he wants to redeem, but he might not get the chance. They must endure the night's passage before an answer comes.

Begin today's study by reading Mark 14:32-41.

Both Boaz and Christ waited through a long night before arriving at a place where they were able to redeem. Both had obstacles standing in their way. Both had people whose lives depended on their ability to save.

What did Jesus ask His disciples to do in verse 38?

God requires different things at different times during our seasons of waiting. Ruth was to rest. The disciples were to watch and pray. Both were to stay by their respective redeemers. Sometimes in our seasons of waiting we are told to cease worrying and tossing, quietly lean on our Savior, and rest. At other times God calls us to actively wait by persisting in prayer and staying keenly alert to our surroundings, ready for whatever appears next. We are always to stay close to our Redeemer.

> Sometimes we are told to quietly lean on our Savior and rest. At other times God calls us to actively wait. But we are always to stay close to our Redeemer.

Read Ruth 3:14-18.

Personal Take: Why do you think Boaz told Ruth not to let anyone know she had come to the threshing floor?

What gift did Boaz give Ruth, and who was it for primarily?

The amount of grain Boaz loaded up in Ruth's shawl is difficult to determine because no specific measurement is given. However, it's safe to say it was somewhere between 58-95 pounds (an unusually large amount). We were all hoping that the weight of fear and anxiety Ruth lugged to the threshing floor could be replaced with a 60-pound bag of grain, I know. Could she not have just one moment without gleaning, toting, and hauling? Where's the spa in this town?

I do wonder how the weight of this grain felt on her back as she plodded back to Naomi's. Was it as feathers under the strength of her newly discovered knowledge of Boaz's love, or did it drag like stones as her future still remained unsettled? I imagine that when Ruth made her way to the threshing floor the previous night, she figured that, good or bad, she would return with an answer. To think that after all she had been through things were still up in the air kind of makes me want to sling her shawl at someone. And, yet, in true Ruth form we see her serving and active in her waiting.

Personal Response: Are you waiting for people, answers, or things? How can you be active as you wait (even if it's a call to intentionally rest)?

Let's catch one more principle today in Matthew 15:29-37. What does this teach about Christ being our supply?

Verse 36 says that Jesus gave the disciples bread, and they, in turn, fed the hungry crowd. How does this principle play out in today's study of Boaz, Ruth, and Naomi?

This convicts and relieves me simultaneously. I can get so spent running around, pouring out of my own paltry resources, and trying to drum something up for the people around me, when all along God has called me to be a deliverer of His gifts, not the creator of them. Yes, Ruth was unflinchingly faithful in coming, going, gleaning, carrying, and delivering, but it all came from Boaz's hand. He alone was her source. Apart from Boaz, Ruth had nothing for herself or to offer Naomi.

Personal Response: In what areas of your life are you tired, spent, and out of resources? Practically speaking, how can you receive the supply you need from Christ?

Today's study really resonated with Alli and Carrie, probably because they have children, though Lauri and Anadara both have one en route. They talked about their children being totally dependent on them, especially Alli's little guy James who's only six weeks old. Their fragile lives literally hang on their parents' ability to provide for them, which from everything I can tell, looks exhausting. Carrie and Alli both mentioned how much more they are aware of their own need to draw from Christ so they can generously pour love and provision on their children.

This can be hard to practice because receiving our supply from God isn't always as tangible as a bag of grain, a fish, or a piece of bread that we walk up and take from His hand. It may be something this concrete, but many times it's a supply of patience, forgiveness, love, wisdom, or comfort that we desperately need from Him so we can pour it out on someone else—just like Ruth did for Naomi with the grain. This kind of spiritual supply comes from being in Jesus' presence. Meditating on the pages of Scripture. Committing to focused prayer. Waiting quietly on Him so our spirits can learn His voice. Ruth knew where Boaz was, she sought him out, and she lay at his feet. It is not surprising she walked away with something to offer someone else.

This week has been emotional for me. I've decided more things get beat on the threshing floor than just grain. Is anyone else with me? I've also decided that blessings so big we can hardly carry them get stored up for us there—often so we can carry them to the bitter, empty, and hungry. Today we looked at our Redeemer who toiled in Gethsemane, a word that means "oil press"—a telling picture of what Jesus would suffer. How interesting that Ruth and Boaz were at a threshing floor where grain is beaten by a flail and Jesus and His disciples were amidst olives that would be crushed for oil. Perhaps both settings are pictures of the cost of redemption. We've looked intently to Boaz this week, but let us not miss our ultimate Redeemer—the One who not only wanted to spread His wings over us but gave His life so He could.

> Our ultimate Redeemer not only wanted to spread His wings over us but gave His life so He could.

CURRY CHICKEN WITH CHICKPEA AND DRIED FRUIT COUSCOUS

PRE-HEAT OVEN TO 350° SERVES 6

CURRY CHICKEN

3 tablespoons olive oil
½ teaspoon salt
2 eggs, beaten
6 chicken breasts

½ cup flour
1 teaspoon curry powder
1 large resealable plastic bag

In a large skillet, heat 3 tablespoons of olive oil. Combine ½ cup flour, ½ teaspoon of salt, and 1 teaspoon curry powder in a large resealable plastic bag. After dipping chicken breasts in bowl with 2 beaten eggs, dredge chicken pieces in flour mixture. Add chicken to skillet and cook over medium-high heat, turning after a few minutes and cooking through. (Note: You can butterfly the chicken breasts to make them thinner and more like chicken tenders. This also makes it go further.) Serve alongside or on top of couscous.

CHICKPEA AND DRIED FRUIT COUSCOUS

3 tablespoons olive oil
1 cup chopped mixed dried fruits
   (apples, pears, apricots, prunes)
2 cups vegetable broth
1 15-oz. can chickpeas,
   drained and rinsed

2 medium onions, chopped
1 teaspoon ground cumin
1½ cups instant couscous
¼ cup chopped scallions
salt

In a large pot, heat oil and sauté onions over medium heat. Add dried fruit and continue cooking for three minutes. Add cumin; continue stirring and cooking for one minute. Add vegetable broth, couscous, and chickpeas. Bring to a boil; cover and turn off heat. Let stand for 5 minutes. Fluff with fork and add salt to taste. Sprinkle with chopped scallions before serving.

MOM'S ICE CREAM DESSERT
SERVES 12 TO 15

This is one I grew up on. If you've never had anything like it, it will be a new staple. Right up there with potatoes or flour.

24 Oreos® (regular, not double stuffed)
½ cup butter (melted)
½ gallon good vanilla ice cream, softened

Directions
Crush Oreos in food processor. Melt butter and stir into crumbs. Press down into 13x9" pan and freeze about 30 minutes. Take out of freezer and spread ice cream on top. Put it back in freezer for an hour or more.

You can then spread commercial fudge sauce over it, but the homemade one is best and easy.

FUDGE SAUCE

2 tablespoons butter
1 cup powdered sugar
I cup semi-sweet chocolate chips
1 5-oz. can evaporated milk
(Or you can substitute commercial fudge sauce)

Melt 2 tablespoons butter, 1 cup powdered sugar, 1 cup semi-sweet chocolate chips with 5 oz. evaporated milk in a pot. Cook gently and whisk until it is all melted and bubbly. Then let cool. Pour it over the frozen ice cream/Oreos and put back in the freezer. The longer it stays in the freezer, the better. Serve and enjoy.

REDEMPTION

I JUST RETURNED FROM A TRIP DOWN THE AMAZON IN BRAZIL.

I SPENT A FULL WEEK ON A BOAT LEARNING THINGS LIKE HOW TO SLEEP IN A HAMMOCK WHILE THE HOLLOW CLICKING OF CAYMANS (BRAZIL'S ALLIGATOR-LIKE SPECIES), THE LOW HUM OF FROGS, AND AN OCCASIONAL ROOSTER WHOSE INNER CLOCK WAS ON A DIFFERENT TIME ZONE ENTIRELY, FOUGHT TO KEEP ME AWAKE AS I SWUNG BACK AND FORTH IN THE NIGHT'S BREEZE. I HAD NEVER SPENT THE NIGHT IN A HAMMOCK BEFORE, BUT THAT WAS JUST ONE OF MANY FIRSTS: I SWAM IN THE AMAZON. I CAUGHT MY FIRST PIRANHA. I ATE MY FIRST PIRANHA. THIS WAS BEFORE MY FRIEND MARY KATHARINE TOLD ME SHE CAUGHT ONE WITH A LEECH CRAWLING OUT OF ITS EYE, WHICH ABRUPTLY ENDED THE PIRANHA PORTION OF MY BRAZILIAN DIET. BACK TO RICE, BEANS, AND 12 TYPES OF BANANAS.

One morning I awoke to our schedule posted on the whiteboard:

6:00 a.m.—Fishing
8:00 a.m.—Breakfast
8:30 a.m.—Devotional
9:30 a.m.—Caboclo House
10:30 a.m.—Acajatuba School (Visit)
3:00-5:00 p.m.—Camp at Nx. De Fatima
7:30 p.m.—Hunting *ALLIGATOR* (emphasis mine)

I wasn't sure if it was just one specific alligator we were hunting or if the plural was lost in translation, but either way, it was that 7:30 p.m. slot that gave me pause. We got rather backed up that day (Brazilian time will do this to you), so we didn't make it out for our big hunt until 10:30. It ended up being a very friendly catch-and-release program, by the way, where the caymans got to get their pictures taken in the boat with Americans. I think they were really happy about this, as evidenced by how quickly they swam away to tell their families about this honor.

Our "hunt" started off a bit slowly as we cast the beams of our flashlights into the reeds looking for cayman eyes (our Western version of deer in headlights). Whenever we spotted two beady reflections, our guides Ulysses and Milton (not making up these names) would shake the light and slowly idle the boat toward the desired specimen when, in an instant, one would try to grab the cayman out of the water and drag it into the boat. This technique failed the first few times, so Milton decided that diving on top of one would be the surest thing. He explained that this was safer than you might imagine because caymans apparently can't open their mouths under water, which most of us found strangely non-relieving. Indeed, he came up with a catch this way, though the rest of us lay passed out in the boat thinking he'd been pulled in by an Anaconda or that he'd jumped on the one mutated cayman in the Amazon that *could* open its mouth under water.

We had loads of fun that night. It was perhaps as exciting as our jungle hike where we saw monkeys and my friend April—who has a really keen eye—accidentally stepped on a boa constrictor, which everyone always says are more afraid of you than you are of them and the only way they'll ever bite you is if you do something like, say, step on them. I held a homemade torch and drank "milk" from a tree; and April wore a rain hat that our guide, Bigode, made her out of a leaf. It kept her drier than the $40 rainproof hat she'd bought in the States. We drank pure, homemade Acai juice, which is supposed to be the healthiest berry in the world and incidentally *tasted* like the healthiest berry in the world. You had to add 14 teaspoons of sugar for it to be drinkable, which then probably classified it as the unhealthiest berry drink in the world.

But more wonderful than the roosters, sky, scorpions, fish, shooting stars, coconuts, and hammocks, were the people. Beautiful, bright, tanned, joyful, glorious people. I had the privilege of meeting these stunning Brazilians who reside in the heart of the jungle because of a brilliant ministry called "Ray of Hope," which brings all manner of aid and the message of Jesus to these precious, yet forgotten, jungle villages along the Amazon. The Villagers left me with images of themselves and their land forever burnished on the walls of my mind. They are a strong and hopeful people. Patient yet always working. They are grateful and content amidst their need and suffering.

As far away as ancient Bethlehem might be removed from the tributaries of the Amazon, I found Scripture amazingly transcendent, thinking of Boaz and Ruth as often as I took in the mission of "Ray of Hope." The people of this ministry have sacrificed their lives, looking for a Ruth in the eyes of every Amazonian they meet. The upper crust has forgotten them, the government has dismissed them, but the Christ followers know a secret: God does not look on the outward appearance of culture, wealth, or status. Rather, He looks for those of noble character who fear Him. And He often uses generous, radically kind people like Boaz to find them, to invite them to the table, to share of their wealth, and, as we'll see this week, to offer them the gift of redemption, as we ourselves have so graciously been given.

And this is not out of pious pity for the lowly, foreigner, and poor, but because we depend on Ruths for our survival. They are the heroes of our faith. The ones whose stories get written in the chronicles of Scripture and in the annals of Heaven. As my dad spoke to the jungle pastors who have given their lives for their people, he said: "Your work will probably not show up in the papers. No one will read about your story in a *New York Times* best seller. Presidents and kings will not know of you. But yours are the truly great stories. The ones celebrated by *the* King."

I wonder if God is calling you to spread your wings over someone. A person who might not look like you, think like you, or shop where you shop. You may not have to go to Africa or Brazil to find them; he or she may live next door or be related to you. Either way, it is time for us to give of our lives as Boaz gave of his. If we clutch our possessions and ease of life, we will do so at the expense of a wealth of Ruths who not only need redemption, but who might one day be the true saviors in our own stories.

DAY 01 REDEMPTION
I WILL, I WON'T

www.livingroomseries.com
Hear the "nogs" talk about what several different elements of the study mean. Kelly also explains about three qualities of a kinsman-redeemer.

We've established a habit of reviewing each chapter we finish, so let's continue it.

Read all of Ruth 3 and note any fresh thoughts below.

Naomi's voice drew last week and chapter 3 to a close: "Wait, my daughter, until you find out what happens. For the man will not rest until the matter is settled today" (v. 18). Last week we pondered this theme of waiting while both Boaz and Ruth had to endure the passage of night, and now we pick up at a moment where Ruth must wait again, the matter totally out of her hands.

While I was on a boat in Brazil, I remember John Paculabo (president of Kingsway Music and a prominent "Ray of Hope" supporter) say something that will stay with me forever. "The people here know how to wait. They wait for clean water. They wait for food. They wait for the floods to recede." They don't resent it. They don't see it as something to rush or dread. Instead, their waiting consists of hopeful endurance secured by a promise they know is on its way.

Even while we're waiting and it seems like nothing is happening, God is still working.

While Naomi and Ruth were in this place of waiting, Boaz was busy at work, reminding me that even while we're waiting and it seems like nothing is happening, God is still working.

Read Ruth 4:1-6 to see how things unfold.

What was the name of the closer relative?

What opportunity did Boaz present to him (vv. 3-4)?

After agreeing to redeem the property, what makes him suddenly change his mind (v. 5)?

If you had difficulty finding the closer relative's name, you're exactly where the narrator wants you. Boaz called him *peloni almoni,* two rhyming Hebrew words that would be something like our *helter-skelter* or *hocus-pocus*. Our closest translation is probably something like "So and So." (Some of your Bibles will say "Such a one.") Perhaps Boaz didn't want to be too friendly to his competition; we can't say for sure, but I thought this was interesting.

There's a lot in these verses foreign to modern-day readers. We don't live in an era of kinsman-redeemers, making much of this difficult to relate to. However, the principles are quite accessible, and I want to focus on them. First, we notice that when Boaz originally pitched the idea of redemption to the closer kinsman, he didn't mention Ruth; he only mentioned property. Property alone (while also presumably providing for Naomi) seemed like such a good deal to him he didn't even have to think about it before agreeing to redeem.

However, Boaz knew of a small caveat—marrying the Moabite widow—which he didn't throw out until after this unnamed redeemer so casually agreed to redeem. This sort of shows a sly side to Boaz, which I really appreciate. It's an attractive move that reminds me of one of my favorite quotes from Anne of Green Gables: "Well, I wouldn't marry anyone who was really wicked, but I think I'd like it if he could be wicked and wouldn't."[1] Though we've seen no wickedness in Boaz, it's nice to know he can unfurl his tricky side when he needs to.

> **Personal Take: Why do you think the caveat of acquiring Ruth was a deal breaker for the nearer kinsman? Study verse 6 and give it some thought.**

Iain Duguid says this about the problematic transaction, "If there were to be a child from the relationship with Ruth, the redeemer would lose the field and there would be no benefit to his own children and estate to compensate for the costs involved in taking care of Naomi and Ruth."[2] So it wasn't just a marriage to Ruth that threw the deal out for this relative. Perhaps the even greater problem was that if Ruth were to bear a child, an heir of Elimilech's, the child would automatically inherit the land this redeemer would have worked so hard to have purchased and maintained. And that's not all—he would have helped to keep Elimilech's line alive, something he was more interested in doing for his own family and legacy.

Although we studied the multifaceted role of kinsman-redeemer *(goel)* on day 5 of session 3, I want to remind you that marriage was *not* part of the required duties. There was, however, another custom in Israelite law called Leverite marriage that may have played into Boaz's proposal to the closer relative. I think the concept is important enough for us to read about in Deuteronomy 25:5-10.

> **After reading this passage, describe in your own words the premise of Leverite marriage.**

The idea of Leverite marriage would have been familiar to Boaz and the closer relative, but since neither of them was Elimilech's immediate brother, marriage to Ruth was not binding on either of them. As mentioned before, the role of a kinsman-redeemer didn't require marriage to the person being redeemed. This makes Boaz's proposition to the *goel,* which included marriage to Ruth quite unique. From what I can understand, the *goel* could have legally purchased the land but passed on Ruth. However, considering the moral obligation to redeem Ruth was put forth by Boaz, the *goel* probably didn't feel comfortable doing less than that. In short, Boaz was after the spirit of what a kinsman-redeemer represented, not merely the letter of its execution. He loved Ruth and wanted her to be redeemed through marriage, something the closer relative was not prepared to do.

We probably can't fault "So and So" too much for refusing to redeem any more than we can fault Orpah for heading back to Moab after Naomi's urging her to return. He was simply making a logical business decision while looking out for his own family and inheritance. On paper, adding Ruth to the deal wasn't profitable or beneficial for him or his descendants, so he simply passed it up. To me, the significance is not what he did wrong but what Boaz did extraordinarily right. The decision of the *goel* not to redeem was reasonable, but when I study Scripture I see that reasonable is not what usually goes down in history.

Personal Response: What sacrificial, scary, risky, or costly decision have you made in obedience to God? And what were the results? (Be honest if it hasn't been easy.)

In the midst of revisiting the role of a kinsman-redeemer and learning about Leverite marriages, we cannot miss the spiritual truth that God does not always call us to the normal or logical. The *goel* did what seemed best for him, much like Orpah did what was best for her, but neither are ever heard from again. In keeping with my Amazon experience, I want to close with a story of a woman who refused to do the logical, the normal, the expected. Her name is Gloria Santos, the founder of "Ray of Hope."

> God does not always call us to the normal or logical.

Gloria spent many years in tourism working as a jungle guide, using the five languages she speaks. After a difficult period in her life, she went to Bible school in Canada and received a word from her teacher that the Lord wanted her to return to the Amazon to work with the children in the jungle. The teacher handed Gloria an envelope containing $200 and told her, "This is for you to start your missionary work, and God will show you the next step."

The only problem was that Gloria was willing to minister anywhere in the world except the Amazon. Although she had grown up there, she had experienced difficult and painful things that caused her to not want to return. She plead with the Lord, "Anywhere but there!" But the Lord kept pressing upon her heart that He wanted to use her back in the jungles of the Amazon. And just a few weeks after her surrender, the Lord faithfully began to change her heart, restoring a joy to return.

One day Gloria's father Joaquim was traveling from the village of Iranduba when a boy with blood on his face ran in front of the car. He took the boy to the hospital, but no one knew who he was. Joaquim returned to the area where he had found the boy and asked a man passing by if he knew him. "I know him. He's Narciso the son of the crazy woman" was the response. The boy lived in a shack in the village, but the family were outcasts. The mother was mentally ill and suffered from epilepsy, and the father was an alcoholic.

Joaquim brought Narciso back to his village and bought a bag of food for the family as they had very little to eat. He returned to his home and spoke with Gloria and his wife Irineia, and they decided to use the $200 that Gloria had been given to help this family. The following weekend Gloria held the first kids camp in this village, and 100 children and 20 parents turned up. At the end of the day, a little girl came to Gloria. "Today was the best day of my life. I have never been so happy. I never knew that someone cared for me, that Jesus cared. Please, when are you coming back?"

Gloria had only intended to do this one camp, but she said, "We'll be back next month. Tell your friends to come." At that moment "Ray of Hope" was birthed. Since then, literally hundreds have come to Christ; and the poor and vulnerable have been fed, helped, and protected. All because one woman decided to answer a call that wasn't logical by human standards.

> **Hundreds have come to Christ ... all because one woman decided to answer a call that wasn't logical by human standards.**

I wonder if your life can be easily explained. If most of your decisions are simply based on what benefits you and your life, I encourage you to note the difference between Boaz and the unnamed *goel*. One did the extraordinary and the other the expected. One chose sacrifice and love while the other chose safety. One left a legacy in the pages of Scripture, the other was never heard from again.

Personal Response: If the Lord is calling you to do the unusual, illogical, or sacrificial, write about it below. And if you long to live such a life, let the Lord know you are willing.

122

DAY 02 REDEMPTION
TO BE WILLING

Last night the "nogs" had dinner at Carrie's—another fabulous meal. Seriously, when's the last time you had mashed potatoes with lemon slices and peas in them (except for when you were a kid and your mom told you that you couldn't leave the table until you ate all your peas so you shoved them into your mashed potatoes cause that's the only way you could finish them without gagging)? But I love peas now, and this was an amazing dish. And strawberries are in season, so Lauri brought her decadent homemade whipped cream along with pound cake. None of this bodes well for weight loss and such, but for just about everything else I find food the perfect accoutrement.

In addition to fine dining, we had equally stimulating conversation. Alli kept our discussion going with this question that perhaps has no definitive answer: "Why did Boaz show Ruth such kindness?"

> **For Discussion: We've been studying their relationship for a few weeks now, so why do you think Boaz showed Ruth kindness?**

In relation to yesterday's study of the unnamed *goel,* I want to highlight three facets of a kinsman-redeemer that will be very important for us today. A kinsman-redeemer must be:

1. Near of kin
2. Able to redeem
3. Willing to redeem

The third qualification is precisely where things for "So and So" fell apart. Yes, he was the closest relative. Yes, he was able to redeem. But we quickly found out that he wasn't willing. And isn't it this third element that often ends up being our downfall? We're able, but so often we're just not willing. This may be one of the most tragic ways for a Christian to spend her life: In the right place with all the right resources but without a willing heart. I so desperately do not want to get to the end of my life to find I've missed having an eternal impact because

> One of the most tragic ways for a Christian to spend her life is to be in the right place with all the right resources but without a willing heart.

I made all of life's decisions based solely on what made sense for me and what was for my benefit—unwilling to yield myself to the Lord.

A great hero of my childhood, Sherry Meddings was a zealous and full-throttle sanguine who eventually succumbed to a long bout with cancer. She used to say, "Lord, may I be willing to be made willing." (This was if you weren't in a willing state or if you weren't even willing to be willing.) The good news, she would always remind us, is that God can change your heart; you just have to be willing to be made willing.

Personal Response: Where are you in your surrender to God? Are you able but unwilling? Write about it below.

Romans 12:1 encourages us to offer our lives to the Lord as living sacrifices. This is something we need not fear; it is the only way to truly live. I used to be afraid of dedicating my life to the Lord, certain that He would seize this small window of opportunity to make my life extraordinarily hard or send me down the Amazon in a hammock (oh, wait). But I am more convinced than ever that it is not yielding my life to the Lord that is the truly awful and frightful place. I long to live the full, adventurous, and impacting life that God desires for me to live. I don't want to miss out on this because I am afraid to entrust myself to Him. Alli feels this is essentially the theme of Ruth's journey. I concur.

Personal Response: If you are willing—or are willing to be made willing—write a prayer of surrender below:

When I think of Ruth's and Naomi's vulnerability, I am reminded of our own powerless state apart from Christ: We were unable to redeem ourselves from the curse of the law, powerless to save ourselves.

How does Romans 5:6 speak to this truth?

We need a Savior who fulfills all three qualities of a kinsman-redeemer. From memory, write the three qualifications:

1. _____

> God can change your heart; you just have to be willing to be made willing.

2. _____

3. _____

Look up the following references and draw a line matching each verse with its corresponding quality.

Mark 10:45   Christ was near of kin (became like us)

Hebrews 2:14-15   Christ was willing to redeem

Hebrews 7:24-25   Christ was able to redeem

How truly amazing that in our powerless, hopeless, sinful state we were given a Redeemer, a Redeemer who left heaven and was made like one of us in human flesh because we needed a Savior who was near of kin. But we needed more than someone related to us. We needed someone who was able to redeem us, and only One qualified for such a task. Because we were bound by the curse of the law we needed someone who was perfect and therefore stood outside the law. And so God gave us a Redeemer who was able. But as we saw yesterday in the character of the closer relative, we would be hopelessly stranded if our redeemer were related and able but unwilling. And here is where Jesus Christ perfectly fulfills the role of kinsman-redeemer: He was not only close and able but He was also lovingly willing.

> Jesus Christ was not only close and able but He was also lovingly willing.

Personal Response: What does Christ's willingness to save you mean to you personally?

Romans 8:1-4: "Therefore, there is now no condemnation for those who are in Christ Jesus, because through Christ Jesus the law of the Spirit of life set me free from the law of sin and death. For what the law was powerless to do in that it was weakened by the sinful nature, God did by sending his own Son in the likeness of sinful man to be a sin offering. And so he condemned sin in sinful man, in order that the righteous requirements of the law might be fully met in us, who do not live according to the sinful nature but according to the Spirit."

DAY 03 REDEMPTION
A NAME

I just had lunch with one of my most introspective friends in Nashville. We both lean to the melancholy and at times overanalytical side of things, so it's always a rip-roaring time when we get together—at least in a hum-drum sort of way. Today we were talking about having impact and having our lives amount to something that really matters. Because she's a songwriter and I'm in the same type of business, there's an added pressure to be commercially successful, for people to know who you are and recognize your name. The mentality is "If you're not getting stopped in the grocery store, what have you really accomplished?" I don't really believe this is true in my heart of hearts, but it feels true when your "success" is measured by numbers, sales, and notoriety, when it's measured by people knowing your name.

Today we're going to read about some not-so-common customs that have to do with people taking off their sandals and giving them away, as well as some other interesting legal proceedings. But mostly we're going to see the importance of a name—though hopefully in a way that's a lot less about fame and more about a name's redemption and preservation. It's such a relief when we're not the ones having to preserve and promote our own names, not to mention just a little more biblical. So start reading, and we'll explore together.

Read Ruth 4:7-10.

What did taking off a sandal and giving it to the other person symbolize in ancient Israel?

Whose property did Boaz purchase, and how did this seem to differ slightly from what he quoted in Ruth 4:3?

**Verse 10 says that Boaz "acquired Ruth the Moabitess."
What is one of the reasons given for why he did this?**

We should note that we've just read the legal proceeding allowing Boaz to purchase Elimilech's property and marry Ruth.* The property purchase and marriage would take place later, but today he was officially recognized as not just a kinsman-redeemer but *the* kinsman-redeemer now that the other *goel* had relinquished his right. This should make us really happy. We've been waiting a long time for this moment, ever since Ruth and Boaz first stumbled upon each other in the middle of a field, which seems like a really long time ago!

If this were a movie, we've reached the part when we grasp for the tissues while our husbands, boyfriends, or friends who are guys go search for what else is playing. Which is exactly why I watched a wedding movie last night with two of my girlfriends and didn't invite one guy over—not that any of them were particularly disappointed, but they just don't typically appreciate these film industry gems.

So let us revel in hearing Boaz proudly say in the presence of witnesses that he was taking Ruth, the Moabitess, Mahlon's widow, to be his wife! I love what Daniel I. Block says about Boaz's proclamation, "The use of the full name … may be required by the legal context, but it is evident that *Ruth's Moabite status is no barrier for Boaz.* On the contrary, perhaps because of her public reputation but especially because of his personal contacts with her, he seems to relish the prospect of marriage to this foreigner" (emphasis mine).[3]

I absolutely love that although Ruth's Moabite heritage might have been a deal breaker for the other *goel,* it was no issue for Boaz. He was proud to acknowledge whom he was marrying, unashamed of who she was before the elders and the townspeople at the city gate. Because I know as women we are plagued with insecurities and pasts that haunt us, I can't pass over this striking symbol of what Christ has done for each one of us and how He knows our full names.

Our heritage is not a deal breaker for Christ.

According to Isaiah 43:1 and John 10:1-3, how are we called?

Read John 20:10-18. At what point did Mary finally recognize Jesus after His resurrection?

I am trying to imagine what it would be like to have Jesus proudly state in the presence of the most honored in my community: "Today I am proud to redeem Kelly Meredith Minter, daughter of Mike and Kay, with her tarnished past, her good days and bad, her brightest and darkest moments. I inherit her qualities, quirks, shortcomings, and sin. I take all of her, and I am delighted to do it!"

Anadara had a similar moment when attending a church of a different denomination than what she was used to. While taking communion, a priest offered her the element of bread as he spoke her name, "Anadara. This is the body of Christ broken for you." The calling of her name, the magnitude and personalization of Christ's willing act for her—Anadara—sent her to tears in a way she had never before experienced during communion.

> **Personal Response: We all have a name, history, and a wake of good and bad. How does Boaz's proclamation of Ruth's name and history as he vowed to redeem her bless you in your understanding of what Christ has done for you? (And do you really believe He takes all of you?)**

In keeping with this theme of names, you noted earlier that one reason Boaz married Ruth was out of a selfless act to preserve Elimilech's name and property (or inheritance). This incredibly noble custom of the Israelites seems far removed from our culture. If no one chose to redeem, Elimilech's name would have forever disappeared from his property and from history, one of the worst things that could have happened to an Israelite. Hubbard explains how Boaz's redemption would prevent this, "The first child born to Ruth and Boaz would own Elimilech's family property and keep him and his sons alive in association with it. ... It ensured that [Elimilech's] name not be cut off ... Hence, his heir ... would look after the deceased's legal rights, especially his 'inheritance' within the community."[4]

In other words, by purchasing Elimilech's land and marrying Ruth, Boaz would selflessly keep Elimilech's name alive and connected with his property. This is an incredible act of *hesed* on Boaz's part just as it is on our part when we think of giving our lives for the fame and longevity of others. Just think how many parents do this for their children and children for their parents!

I started today by writing about my own desire to have impact and to have a name that matters, and I've discovered this happens in a way that is mostly countercultural. Instead of having to promote our names through fame and success, we see in Scripture that we have been called by God by name. This very fact gives indefinable value to our names. In addition, we see that in sacrificing his life to preserve Elimilech's name, it was actually Boaz's name that has been preserved through history for countless generations.

We have been called by God by name.

Personal Response: What meant the most to you in today's study? Write your response here.

*Note: For historical accuracy, it's important to understand that Naomi was not technically selling her property. As a widow she did not technically own Elimilech's land. Rather, this exercise allowed Boaz the legal right to Elimilech's property, per Naomi's presumed consent.

DAY 04 REDEMPTION
A BLESSING

I'm really intrigued by our verses today. They are a collective blessing from the witnesses whose message we'll study, though the idea of spoken blessing is of equal importance. It doesn't seem as if we speak a lot of blessings over one another as much these days. We wish and hope for people, but I don't know that we pronounce blessings over them. Maybe it happens more in charismatic circles, but I haven't experienced a lot of spoken blessings in my life, though it's something I believe in, and this passage has made me think about it more deeply.

My hunch is that wherever you are at this moment you could use a spoken blessing. And I'm not talking about random happy wishes that someone sprinkles over you like fairy dust. I'm talking about Spirit-led, biblical words that implore the power of Yahweh over your life in a purposeful manner. This is a biblical practice that the people of Israel employed with Ruth and Boaz that I think you'll find inspiring.

> My hunch is that wherever you are at this moment you could use a spoken blessing.

Read Ruth 4:11-12.

How did the witnesses refer to Ruth? Circle your answer.

the Moabitess   the widow

the Woman   the daughter-in-law

What two women did they want Ruth to resemble?

To fully understand this unique blessing, we have to understand who they're talking about. For the ancient Israelites, names such as *Rachel, Leah, Tamar, Judah,* and even *Perez* would have been familiar, but it probably wouldn't hurt us to dig into who these people are.

Read more about Rachel and Leah in Genesis 29:14–30:24. This seems like a lot, but it's quite exciting and dramatic. Don't worry, you can do a really quick survey. Feel free to skim.

130

Personal Take: After briefly reading about Rachel's and Leah's lives, why would the people of the court have wanted Ruth to resemble them? (There's a hint in Ruth 4:11.)

Genesis 49 gives an account of 12 of Rachel's and Leah's (and their maidservants') children concluding with, "All these are the twelve tribes of Israel" (v. 48). When we look at this history, we begin to understand how unprecedented, staggering, and massive the witnesses' blessing was over Ruth. In essence, they were calling for a widowed, childless Moabitess to be blessed with the kind of fertility given to Rachel and Leah who had many and particularly distinguished children—the ones who built up the house of Israel. This is absolutely huge! Not only was Ruth being embraced by Israel as a true Israelite, but they were looking for her to play a prominent role in their society and legacy. This should give us tremendous hope that God can delight in using us, no matter our culture or histories.

> God delights in using us, no matter our culture or histories.

Personal Response: How does the witnesses' blessing on Ruth change the way you see God's ability to redeem your past?

Let's look at just a few more people to fully appreciate the blessing of the elders and the townspeople. Hopefully, you remember Judah from day 3 of session 2. He was the father of the tribe of Judah from which both Elimilech and Boaz descended. Judah had a son named Perez by a woman named Tamar, someone who played a very important role in the line of Judah.

Tamar's story is in Genesis 38. I know this is a lot of reading, but do another brief survey of her life in this chapter.

Who was Perez and what was unique about his birth (vv. 27-30)?

Since Tamar had also been widowed before having children (yet later bore Perez to Judah), the witnesses may have been highlighting her as the inspiration for how God could also bless Ruth with a child who could impact Israel's future. Not to mention, her descendents through Perez played a most significant role in Israel's history and were the ancestors that made up Boaz's clan living in Bethlehem.

If all this is confusing, let me sum things up: The people of Bethlehem wanted Ruth to be like Rachel and Leah because their children built up the house of Israel. They wanted Boaz's line to be like that of Perez who was born to Judah and Tamar, because this was the clan Boaz descended from. (It's just the tiniest bit like someone blessing you for being from Illinois, then more specifically blessing you for being from Chicago, if that helps you at all).

I know this has been a heavy day of reading and learning more about the 12 tribes of Israel and how all kinds of hardship from deceit to prostitution played a role in its formation. So I want to end on a lighter note, one that will pick up nicely from yesterday's study on the preservation of someone's name. Ruth 4:12 finds the witnesses blessing Boaz with standing and fame in Bethlehem. How ironic that Boaz's decision to preserve someone else's name (Elimilech's), turned into his own fame and recognition. His sacrificial redemption of Naomi and Ruth proved to make a lasting name for him as long as Scripture endures. Perhaps this is just a little of what it means in Luke 9:24 when Jesus says, "For whoever wants to save his life will lose it, but whoever loses his life for me will save it."

Laying down our lives for others, for the sake of Jesus, is never wasted.

You may be laying your life down for your children or maybe for your husband. Perhaps you're about to get married and enter an altogether new level of self-sacrifice. Or maybe you're single and you're giving your life to friendships, family, and ministries. Maybe you've been asked to take care of your parents, or you've taken in a family member, or you've adopted a child. All I know is that laying down our lives for others, for the sake of Jesus, is never wasted. No matter how quiet, how humble, how thankless, God is making a name for you—one that will last an eternity. Go in the sweetness of this truth.

DAY 05 REDEMPTION
A WEDDING, A BABY

Begin by reading Ruth 4:13 and then come back to me 'cause we need to talk.

Ruth 4:13
Boaz took Ruth and she became his wife. Then he went to her, and the LORD enabled her to conceive, and she gave birth to a son.

I am pro-men. Really. But what in the world? This is the moment we've been waiting for, the huge pay-off; and our distinctly male narrator comes out with a marriage, a pregnancy, and the birth of a son that's crammed into a tiny verse like he's rattling off a grocery list. Could we not linger, tarry, relish for just one moment? Would it be so wrong to give each of these life-altering events its very own verse? Could we get a little wedding detail, news of the pregnancy, and the parents' reaction to having a son? I mean, when we're told things like how many pounds of barley Ruth could carry, would it kill us to know what kind of dress she wore, who her flower girl was?

I'm actually a to-the-point kind of a person, but even I feel rushed by verse 13. I think we need to brood over these details a bit; these are answers to prayer, and these remarkable twists need a little acknowledgment and consideration.

For Discussion: What do you think of this news? Does is surprise you? Does it make you hopeful in your own life?

I want to look at these three stages individually because I think you'll be really blessed by studying them and because I'm not afraid to squeeze blood from a turnip.

Fill in the blank: "So Boaz took Ruth and she became his _____."

Hubbard says one of the coolest things I've ever seen, "She had socially ascended from 'foreigner' (2:10), through 'maidservant' (2:13) and 'maiden' (3:9), to 'wife'."[5] I can't tell you what this means to me, as we see in a sentence how God has drastically changed Ruth's life. He didn't do it overnight. Each stage slowly gave way to the next, her faithfulness and loyalty yielding each new promotion and season of life. What an inspiration to keep going knowing that God will give the increase.

I wrote my first Bible study about modern-day idols and called it, *No Other Gods*. One of the main characteristics of serving false gods is that we must constantly downgrade our expectations of them. We start with high hopes and dreams that a certain idol will deliver happiness, excitement, and well-being to our lives; but because a false god is false by its very nature, our expectations must continually be lowered until we're in total bondage to something that doesn't even resemble anything close to what we had originally hoped. But not so with the one true God. With Him we find the opposite. The more we get to know Him, the more we trust and serve Him, the more our expectations ascend and our realities bloom.

> **Personal Response: Ruth has been described as the Moabitess, the foreigner, and the woman beneath the servant girls. Now she is a celebrated wife and a true Israelite. How has God changed your life? What has He brought you from? (Don't skip this because it takes thought and heart. Spend time with God.)**

> **Verse 13 mentions a third individual besides Boaz and Ruth. Who was it and how did the individual intervene?**

This is a really interesting mention and only the second time the Lord is shown directly intervening in the whole Book of Ruth.

> **Look back at 1:6b. What was the first instance?**

The Lord shows Himself directly involved in this moment. It's not that He hasn't been maneuvering and working throughout the entire story, but the direct mention of His enabling Ruth to conceive is a big deal, especially since we know Ruth was married to Mahlon for presumably 10 years with no children. Though quickly referenced, this is a miracle.

> **Several references in Scripture show God's hand in conception. Look up the following references and name the corresponding woman next to each verse:**

134

Genesis 29:31 _____

Genesis 30:22 _____

I Samuel 1:19-20 _____

Luke 1:24-25 _____

Personal Take: Out of all the opportunities for the narrator to have inserted God's direct hand, why do you think he chose to do it in reference to Ruth's conception?

We've looked at Ruth's marriage and pregnancy, and now I want to close by looking at the significant birth of her son, whose name has not yet been revealed. That God would choose to bless Ruth with a child, especially after her inability to bear one with Mahlon, is an incredible treasure in and of itself. But as we've looked at the ramifications of legacy through descendents in Israel's history, we appreciate this child as having even further significance.

Look back at Ruth 1:11-13. What was Naomi's biggest reason for persuading Ruth and Orpah to return to Moab?

This is such good medicine for those of us who can only think of one way for a particular situation to be resolved. Naomi saw herself as the only way to procure another husband for Ruth, and therefore a son. Since she was too old, she wrote the whole thing off. It never occurred to Naomi that Ruth would bear her own Israelite child who would one day be Naomi's redeemer. It is true that we just can't think on the plane of God; our minds are unable to comprehend His ways (Isa. 55:9). And I find this encouraging when my brain shorts out on solutions and I'm discouraged because I can't understand my own way.

> We just can't think on the plane of God; our minds are unable to comprehend His ways.

Read Ruth 2:11-12. List all the ways Yahweh answered Boaz's prayer by repaying Ruth for all she had done.

Ruth has given birth to a son. She has lost, she has loved, and now she is leaving a legacy. Through this son she will save Elimilech's name from being forever lost. She will preserve Naomi's own legacy, which had been hanging on by a doomed thread since her husband and sons died in the dreaded land of Moab. Through this child she will give Boaz a great name and fulfill the blessing the elders and witnesses spoke over him—that he would have great standing and fame throughout Bethlehem. And through this son she will preserve her own name as one who, indeed, will help build up the house of Israel. And this is just the beginning …

Next week we will look at the incomprehensible reaches of her legacy, a blessing that has extended to this very day and no doubt will extend to the very end of time and into eternity. Let us not forget that it all began with a woman who left her home to live in the land of the God under whose wings she had come to take refuge. I imagine every true legacy begins this way.

> **Personal Response: This week we've talked about stepping out in faith, being willing (or willing to be made willing), believing that we can trust God with our future and that He knows our full name. Alli has encouraged us to have a closing prayer time over the one thing that touched you most this week.**

LOVE CHANGES EVERYTHING

Anadara Arnold & Kelly Minter
See the story behind the song at www.livingroomseries.com.

Once upon a winter's moon
All I loved was lost too soon
But hope was hiding just below
The coldness of the melting snow
I was afraid, I was undone
But you saw my face and it carried me on

Chorus
Love is moving, fluttering through me
Springtime's riding in on the wind
The clouds are breaking, my heart's awakening
Cause love changes everything

Once upon a harvest moon
You twirled me like a flower in bloom
You knelt beneath the satin sky
I took your hand and made it mine
What have I done that I would deserve
To be the one to forever be yours

Chorus
Love is sounding, echoing round me
Springtime's riding in on the wind
The birds are singing, bells are ringing
Cause love changes everything

Bridge
Love changes everything
La, la, la, la, la la
Love changes everything

Kelly Minter & Anadara Arnold. MintyFresh Music (ASCAP) Postage Stamp Publishing/ASCAP, Administered by The Loving Company

To purchase this song or CD go to
www.LifeWay.com/livingroomseries.

CLASSIC LASAGNA WITH HOMEMADE NOODLES

PRE-HEAT OVEN TO 350° SERVES 6

CLASSIC LASAGNA

1 lb. lasagna noodles (or homemade)
16 oz. cottage cheese
3 cloves garlic
2 lbs. ground beef
½ teaspoon oregano (dried)
1 can tomato paste
4 tablespoons Worcheshire sauce
1 tablespoon Heinz 57® Sauce (optional)

1½ lbs. mozzarella cheese
4 tablespoons olive oil
1 large onion, chopped
1 teaspoon basil (dried)
dash nutmeg
4 cups whole canned tomatoes
1 tablespoons A-1® Steak Sauce

Brown onion and garlic in olive oil. Add meat and cook until done. Drain grease. Add oregano, basil, nutmeg, and sauces. Add tomato paste, tomatoes, and enough tomato juice to fill the tomato paste can. Simmer uncovered for one hour or till liquid is cooked off. Add cottage cheese. Layer in 9x13" pan starting with noodles then sauce then cheese, making 4 layers (12 noodles). Finish with cheese. Bake at 350° for 20 minutes.

HOMEMADE NOODLES

1 cup semolina flour
1 cup all-purpose flour
2 tablespoons olive oil

⅓ cup water
2 large eggs

Process flours in food processor for 30 seconds. In a bowl, whisk water, eggs, and olive oil. With processor running, add liquid through the shoot. Process until a round ball appears. Kneed lightly about five times. Cover with plastic wrap and let sit for 30 minutes.

Boil 6 quarts water with 1 tablespoon salt. Separate dough into 13 balls and cover in plastic. Remove one at a time and place on lightly floured surface. Roll into 3x13" strips. Set covered on a lightly floured surface. Lower 1-3 noodles at a time into boiling water. Cook 90 seconds or until done. Remove with slotted spoon. Repeat until all are done. Then follow lasagna directions above.

INSALATA ESTIVA
SERVES 6-8

I ate this at a restaurant in San Francisco and duplicated it for a dinner party. It's a different dish but made with all your trusted favorites.

1½ quarts (6 cups) cherry tomatoes, all colors
4 oz. mozzarella cheese, cubed
15 big basil leaves
¼ cup capers (or more to taste*)
1 small red onion
4 tablespoons red wine vinegar
2 tablespoons olive oil
pepper
salt

Directions
Wash cherry tomatoes and slice in half across. Put them into a salad bowl and heavily salt them. Set aside while you're preparing the rest of the ingredients. Wash fresh basil. Roll up each leaf and slice into strips. Cut strips in half if they're too long. Dice red onion. Slice four ounces of mozzarella cheese into bite-sized cubes. Add basil, onion, mozzarella, and capers to salted tomatoes in salad bowl. Add vinegar and oil. Add pepper to taste and toss.

*Note from Kelly: I actually used ½ cup of capers. You might want to start with less and then add more if you really like them.

I ALWAYS KNEW THE DAY WOULD COME, BUT I WAS NO LESS SURPRISED WHEN IT ACTUALLY HAPPENED.

I REMEMBER DRIVING TO A REHEARSAL ON A SATURDAY MORNING WHEN MY MOM CALLED TO TELL ME THAT MY GRANDFATHER ON MY DAD'S SIDE HAD PASSED AWAY. IT WOULD BE ONLY A FEW SHORT WEEKS LATER, ON THE SAME DAY OF THE WEEK, THAT I'D GET THE SAME NEWS ABOUT MY GRANDMOTHER. AND JUST A FEW MONTHS AFTER THAT WOULD I GET A CALL FROM MY DAD SAYING MY OTHER GRANDFATHER, AFFECTIONATELY KNOWN AS POP, HAD LEFT US TOO—RIGHT AT THE BEGINNING OF A STRING OF WINS FOR THE CRIMSON TIDE (HE WAS A TIRELESS ALABAMA FAN). I THINK HE FIGURED THAT AFTER THEIR FIRST VICTORY THEY'D BE OK WITHOUT HIM.

It was a lot of loss in a short amount of time, the culmination of all their lives making me muse about the meaning of legacy. Especially as I mourned with children, grandchildren, and fussy great-grandchildren who were too young to know someone profoundly important had left them. This was never more apparent then when my niece Maryn and all her baby cousins were sucking and beating on the back of the historic wooden pews of the United States Naval Academy Chapel. The funeral of my dad's father, Charles S. Minter, took place there, and he wouldn't have wanted it any other way—a chamber of people made up of distinguished military guests and drooling grandbabies precisely captured his spirit.

The gravity of that day is unforgettable. Pulling onto the Academy grounds on a brilliant spring morning brought back memories of the drive I made many times with my grandfather. He used to point in the general direction of the cemetery and say with dry cynicism, "One of these days you'll put me in the ground over there, and I'll be just a fond memory." I'm not sure he ever thought too much about the actual day of his funeral: the full military honors, the myriad admirals who would be in attendance, including the Joint Chief of Staff flanked with swords and secret servicemen, the exquisite Navy band, the thundering canons, or the 21 shots that rang out over the Severn River bullet by bullet.

He may never have grasped the full weight of what his life meant, though never did I see this towering bulwark of a man cry except at family gatherings when he gave the blessing over his ever-expanding brood. Legacy he understood.

I remember standing in the front of the chapel that day, overwhelmed at the prospect of trying to take everything in. My eyes drifted from the Navy ship hanging from the rafters, to the casket draped by the American flag, and over to the blazing white uniforms of the men who tended him. I listened to admirals testify about his life and let my eyes flood with all the blue and gold they could hold. I sang the hymns with broken gusto until my voice fully gave way to sobs somewhere in the middle of "A Mighty Fortress Is Our God." What is it about these old hymns that tether you to the past while anchoring you in the hope of heaven—they have that indefinable quality.

Somewhere in my grief and celebration I had the simple but profound realization: My grandfather had given his life—his whole life—to the Navy. And it was in that same moment that I determined if I were ever going to be truly great like him, if I were ever going to leave a noble legacy, I would have to give my life—my whole life—to the Lord.

After the memorial service and burial, we had a festive celebration of my grandfather's life at the superintendent's mansion. I share his love of Chesapeake Bay shrimp and crab, so I had little problem devouring the seafood … and chocolate, and delicately sliced fruit, and fried little tastings, and fizzy drinks in his honor. It would have killed him to see Navy money "wasted" on his behalf, but we all knew better, and this was the one time we could overrule him. It was in this mingling environment where several wise and prominent people approached me and said, "You'll never attend another funeral like this in your lifetime." After experiencing that day, I imagine they're right.

My grandfather was a retired admiral who served in three wars and held the position of superintendent of the Naval Academy, along with being honored as a distinguished graduate from the Academy. He was a pilot and a skipper, the *Intrepid* being one of the ships he commanded. But, if you asked him, these were not his greatest accomplishments. He was a man of unparalleled integrity. He was generous, supportive, and loyal. He was humble—unless you were playing golf and then that was another matter. He loved his wife. He loved his children. He adored his grandchildren and great-grandchildren. And we loved and revered him in return.

Without doing a thing to deserve it, I've been privileged to sail behind him, skimming along in the wake he so carefully carved for 92 years. He modeled life for me, taught lessons, told stories, and gave gifts that have made life's ride so much smoother and richer. His impeccable character, sophisticated humor, passion for athletics, high-strung ways, his love for the Navy—all of it's shaped me, though thank goodness I skirted the Minter nose.

At its simplest, I've been given a stunning heritage I did nothing to earn; and that's the beauty of legacy. It's a gift we leave for others.

Proverbs 17:6 says that grandchildren are the crown of grandparents and that parents are the glory of their children—something we will see this week as we discover the amazing names that descend from Ruth and Boaz. And as we learn about these remarkable people, we'll better grasp their astounding legacy, because you can never separate legacy from people. Or from football, I'm pretty sure.

So Pop, if you can hear me—Roll Tide!

And, Grandma and Grandpa, I'm pretty sure this has already been settled in heaven, but Beat Army!

> Grandchildren are the crown of grandparents,
>
> and parents are the glory of their children.
>
> PROVERBS 17:6, GOD'S WORD TRANSLATION

DAY 01 LEGACY
NAOMI

www.livingroomseries.com Kelly talks about the importance of legacy.

There's a quality about the close of something that can be both simultaneously rewarding and sad, which is the measure of ambivalence I feel as I embark on this last week of study. Of course it will be nice to recapture my life from the realms of Bethlehem and barley, where I've lived for the past several months, but I will miss waking up thinking about you and how the story is shaping your heart. I hope you will miss the journey too, as you can probably tell that the few remaining verses in the Book of Ruth are dwindling and the story line is drawing to a close. There's only one more recipe to try or destroy your kitchen with, depending on your culinary outlook. And if you're anything like Lauri, you peeked ahead and noticed we have mostly genealogies left, which terrified you and greatly diminished your desire to finish. But some of the most interesting twists in our story remain to be plucked out of that genealogical hat—where an otherwise boring list of names will turn into redemption's greatest story. Seriously, you're going to love it.

Some of the most interesting twists in our story remain to be plucked out of that genealogical hat.

Before we get there, I hope you feel great accomplishment, knowing that for the past five weeks you've given yourself to studying one of the most remarkable women in Scripture while, more importantly, opening your heart up to her God. (And if you made Anadaras's Indian couscous with chickpeas, you should feel darn proud as well.)

Personal Response: Ask God to prepare your heart for this week of study and then read Ruth 4:14-15.

Who suddenly takes center stage and does this surprise you?

After last week's remarkable events of a marriage between Ruth and Boaz, their ensuing pregnancy, and birth of a son, I wasn't particularly expecting verse 14 to pick up with all things Naomi. I more anticipated her character to flicker off into the distance while the story tied its final bow around Ruth and Boaz. Instead, we find the narrator doing quite the opposite, drawing these two out of the book's final scene while casting the light back on Naomi and the new child.

SESSION 06 LEGACY

Personal Take: Considering the whole book, why do you think Naomi got such significant billing here at the end of the story?

Who spoke to Naomi in verses 14-15?

You might remember them from Ruth 1:19-20. Look back at these verses and note how Naomi responded to them here.

I kind of like that no specific names are given, just the elusive "women." Because the reality is that we all know exactly who they are. They are the women we grew up with, the thick-as-thieves church moms who were there when we were born, performed ridiculous skits at our church retreats, helped us celebrate our birthdays, wrote us a big check for graduation, cried at our weddings (or are crying because we haven't had a wedding yet). They're the ones who still come scrambling down the church aisle to squeeze the breath out of us when we visit home, and to find out if we've met someone ... and if there's going to be a wedding. I love these women! They're the Mrs. Mitchell's, Mrs. Wolfe's, Mrs. Wiegold's, Mrs. Hardy's. They're, you know, the *women!*

And if you didn't grow up in a church environment, you still had women. They were your mom's closest friends and distant friends—the people who colored your childhood and surrounded you. In Naomi's case they were the ones who jumped up and down and caused the whole town to stir with excitement over her return (because only women can make an entire town go nuts). And they were the ones Naomi felt comfortable enough with to yell, "Don't call me Naomi! Call me a bitter old woman because God has made my life miserable!" These are those women. The same ones who wept when Naomi left Bethlehem, rejoiced when she returned, probably gossiped about her after she flipped out, are now gathered around her at the birth of her grandson, speaking words of blessing over her. I would have liked to have gotten in on some of this, actually, because church moms know how to speak some blessing—even conservative ones.

For Discussion: If you were Naomi, what part of the women's blessing would have meant the most to you and why (vv. 14-15)?

How intriguing that the rim of the spotlight has moved from encircling Ruth and Boaz, where we anticipated it to stay, to shining back on Naomi, this time finding her heart and fortune remarkably transformed. When you consider that the book is named after Ruth and that she tends to twinkle as the story's star, one expects it to begin and end with her. We find instead that the narrator begins with Naomi and returns to her in the final scene. I want to follow this divinely inspired direction and explore a bit further. So we can better appreciate Naomi's newly celebrated position, let's look at some defining stages of her life.

Next to each reference jot down a few words that describe her position or place (I filled in some for you).

1:1-2 Naomi moved to Moab because of a famine.

1:3

1:5

1:6

1:11 Naomi urged her daughters-in-law to not go with her.

1:20-21

2:18

3:1-4 Naomi schemed to get Ruth and Boaz together.

3:18

4:9

Personal Response: How does Ruth 4:14-15 reveal God's heart toward the sufferer?

Does this unlikely redemption change the way you view God's heart? If so, how?

This is really important because this very purposeful focus on Naomi at the close of the story is not what most of us expect. Linear thinking would say it's one thing for Ruth's life to be restored and celebrated because we all kind of get the sense that she deserved it. But it's another thing to see God's immeasurable blessing poured out on Naomi because she hasn't always been the most worthy character. No matter how much we say we believe in grace, we still like things to follow a certain pattern: The good sacrificial servant girl should get top billing in the final scene and the sometimes ornery mother-in-law shouldn't get to hog the baby and the spotlight.

But grace stuns our theories and carefully constructed notions of how things should go. It blesses those who don't deserve it, redeems names that would otherwise have disappeared, and sets glory in the bosoms of once-forsaken widows.

The story could easily have ended by highlighting the exceptional stars, Ruth and Boaz. But I believe the curtain closing on Naomi, encircled by a rejoicing community, holding a grandson she never imagined, while resting in a secured future was divinely deliberate. Yes, Yahweh rewarded Ruth and Boaz for their extraordinary obedience, but He also blessed and redeemed a woman who had lived in a land far from Him and who returned in deep bitterness. And *she's* the one the story ends with!

Why? Because Yahweh is the true hero of the story and unmerited favor is His specialty. While we were still sinners, Christ died for us (Rom. 5:8). He seems to operate this way, and I am so thankful because if I'm honest, I am much more of a Naomi at heart than I've ever been a Ruth. Perhaps nothing makes me happier than to see this lovely story leave its crown upon Naomi's gray head. It's just like God to do that.

Personal Response: Close today's study by meditating on Psalm 103:8-10, thanking God for His grace.

> No matter how much we say we believe in grace, we still like things to follow a certain pattern. ... But grace stuns our theories and carefully constructed notions of how things should go.

DAY 02 LEGACY
A KING IS COMING

Writing this study has stirred me in ways I didn't expect. When I started to immerse myself in the Book of Ruth, I was thinking along the lines of long journeys, single women who knew how to make things happen, and God's redemption. I wasn't planning for the wrestling and wondering I would experience after a long love story, a marriage, and now a child. For someone who is single, these are not easy topics to dwell on day after day. In fact, this must be why I drowned myself in my zillionth viewing of *Sleepless in Seattle* the other night. I think most every girl hopes there's someone out there for her, whether he's a rich landowner who threshes barley or an architect from Seattle who flies to the Empire State Building to find her—because the two of them together will be, undoubtedly, magic.

And don't even get me started on legacy. When you start encroaching on a certain decade, you wonder if you'll ever experience the miracle of bearing a child—if you'll have a little brood to watch at t-ball games, to pick up from Sunday School, and to teach the art of ice cream cone licking. Tonight I fed applesauce and diced pizza to Finley (Carrie's two-year-old), and it was one of the better moments of my day. "I need moe peesa keh-eeh!" with a full mouth. (See, adorable.) Please don't misunderstand. I thoroughly enjoy my life and am blanketed by a dynamic community while doing things I absolutely love. And, yes, I believe I can still leave a legacy without flesh-and-blood offspring, but my sentiments are honest offerings, so I thought I would record them especially for the women who might feel just a bit the same way.

Read Ruth 4:16-17.

We're finally told the name of Ruth's son. What is it?

You may be asking yourself why this group of women was naming Ruth's son. Interestingly, this is the only example in the Old Testament where someone other than the child's parents is recorded naming the child. Some scholars argue that the women were merely affirming the name that Ruth, Boaz, or Naomi had already given him. Regardless, this scene is one-of-a-kind in the Old Testament.

A similar example is in Luke 1:57-60. Read these verses and note the one significant difference below.

Ruth 4:16 notes that Naomi took the child in her lap (or against her breast) and cared for him. We're not certain of the details, but it appears Ruth allowed Naomi a significant role in raising Obed, perhaps something similar to a foster mother. Though not a legal move, Ruth's great affection for (and not obligation to) Naomi allowed her an intimate place in caring for Obed.

Fill in the blank: "For your daughter-in-law who _____ _____ has given him birth" (Ruth 4:15).

Ruth's incredible act of *hesed* in granting Naomi such a close-knit bond with her child reminds me of Hannah's story with her son Samuel.

Read Hannah's prayer in 1 Samuel 1:10-11.

What did she promise to do if God gave her a son?

Both Ruth and Hannah's remarkable unselfishness with their children shines brightly against many Old Testament stories of prominent women often characterized by bitter fighting and jealousy when it comes to bearing children. We get a strong sense that Ruth wanted her beloved mother-in-law to have a significant role in Obed's life, that it deeply blessed Ruth to see the once hopeless Naomi rocking the child against her breast as if he were her own. And this is so different from some of the other stories we read in Scripture and what we encounter in our own modern lives. When it comes to something we desperately want, our propensity is to clutch and protect; the last thing we sometimes think of is how we can bless God or someone else with our coveted treasure.

> The last thing we sometimes think of is how we can bless God or someone else with our coveted treasure.

When speaking at women's events, I notice a common theme of mothers who struggle to release their children to the Lord.

Personal Response: If you have children, is releasing them to the Lord difficult for you? If you don't have children, what is another relationship you have a hard time entrusting to God?

The meaning of Obed's name is not explained in the text, which is unusual when compared to other Old Testament naming practices. We do know that *Obed* is an abbreviated version of *Obadiah,* meaning "servant of Yahweh," but the name *Obed* is a bit more ambiguous, simply meaning "to serve" or "one who serves." It seems possible that he was given this name because he would ultimately serve Naomi by restoring her life and taking care of her in her old age.

This makes sense if you look back at 4:15a. What did the women say this child would specifically do for Naomi?

Children have a way of refreshing our lives like nothing else. Since Alli just gave birth to her son, James, I asked her to write about how this tiny bundle of life has renewed her own:

> *Sometimes when I look at James, I think that this is the closest I will ever get to God. It's something in his newness that is so peaceful to me. It's like he came straight from the Father, a gift that I will never deserve but will cherish with every part of me. From the first time they laid him on my chest, it was as if a chamber of my heart that had been there dormant came to life. Like I am just now beginning to learn how to love.*

Though there's nothing else written about Obed in the Bible, we know that he revived Naomi's heart from loss and hopelessness. We also know about his remarkable descendants, which make him a hugely significant player in biblical narrative.

Fill in the blanks below:

"He was the father of _____ , the father of _____" (v. 17).

Children have a way of refreshing our lives like nothing else.

The Book of Ruth has had many surprising twists and bends in its four short chapters, but this may be the most shocking bit of news yet. We have just learned of Obed's descendents, discovering that he would be the grandfather of King David! In just a few short words the story has suddenly gone from being a quaint love story between two people in the small town of Bethlehem to a national plan of redemption not only for Ruth and Naomi but also for all of Israel and beyond. This surprise revelation changes absolutely everything and affirms that the women's blessing was more accurate than they ever could have imagined.

> **Go back and read 4:14b. How do we see the women's blessing of Obed now fulfilled?**

We'll dig into the ramifications of this revelation later this week, but mull over one thing as you go … Remember this bit of news was implemented into the story many years after Ruth's death. When Ruth gave birth to Obed, she had no idea that a ruddy little shepherd boy named David was on his way. She knew nothing about an unparalleled genius named Solomon, or any other descendants for that matter. What she knew was faithful obedience and love to God during her earthly years would affect things long after she was gone, even if she never got to see how.

> Faithful obedience and love to God during our earthly years can affect things long after we are gone.

> **"These all died in faith, not having received the promises, but having seen them afar off, and were persuaded of them, and embraced them, and confessed that they were strangers and pilgrims on the earth" (Heb. 11:13, KJV).**

> **Personal Response: Spend time speaking to God and listening to Him about your own legacy. Write any thoughts you have below.**

DAY 03 LEGACY
THE HEART

I wish you could personally meet the "nogs" 'cause so much of what they have to say can only be fully appreciated in tandem with their distinctive personalities. Anadara exudes this principle, her oft astounding predicaments cannot be separated from the fact that they always happen to her. And not just predicaments but random scenarios that end up being orchestrated blessings, side-splitting stories—or both.

A couple of winters ago Anadara and her husband, Rocky—see, it's things like having a husband named *Rocky* that I'm talking about—bought a house they planned to renovate. With their eye on architecture and interior aesthetics, tending to the outside was the last thing on their minds.

But in true Anadara form and unknown to her, a slew of perfectly positioned flowers hid beneath the ground, poised to break the surface at spring's cue. Peonies, irises, roses, begonias, and all manner of perennials sprang up, adding their voices to the garden's ensemble as the weather warmed. The previous owner had left a landscaping legacy for Anadara and her husband, though I'm sure she wasn't thinking about them when she seeded, watered, plotted, and pruned. Nonetheless, her skillful gardening left something far beyond what only she would enjoy.

As we look at the following genealogy, try not to approach it as a dry list of odd-sounding names; rather, think of it as a little flower garden that's sprung up since the days of Perez. He had no idea what amazing families and names would come after him—nor do we always know our own legacies.

> **Read Ruth 4:18-22. (We're at the end. I'm having a moment here.)**
>
> **The list begins with Perez. Briefly write what you already know about Perez, being sure to include who his father was. (Go back to session 5, day 4 if you need a reminder.)**

We know little about Hezron and Ram and not a great deal about Amminadab except that he was the father-in-law of the significant high priest, Aaron (Ex. 6:23). His son, Nahshon, was a major leader of the tribe of Judah, and his son, Salmon (of whom not much is known), was the father of Boaz. Of course, we know Boaz was the father of Obed, and, as we saw yesterday—here's where things really get interesting— the son of Obed was Jesse, and the son of Jesse was David.

> **Read 1 Samuel 16:1 and fill in the blank (we read this verse in session 4, but we're coming at it from a different angle today).**
>
> **God sent Samuel to Jesse of _____.**

For years I learned about Scripture in compartments: Adam and Eve in the garden, Noah and the ark, Daniel and the lion's den, Mary and Joseph in the stable, Paul on the road to Damascus … Meditating on single stories has its benefits, but it's always richer when we can see their place in the greater whole of Scripture. Which is why I get excited that the Book of Ruth ends with a genealogy, of all things, because it ties Ruth, Boaz, and Naomi's smaller story into the much greater one— reminding us that our own stories too are part of a divine whole.

That's why I wanted you to note that Samuel was sent to Jesse of Bethlehem, because that immediately ties us back to how the Book of Ruth began: "And a man from Bethlehem in Judah, together with his wife [Naomi] and two sons, went to live for a while in the country of Moab." It reminds us that generations before Jesse of Bethlehem was born, his great great-grandparents (Elimilech and Naomi) ventured off to Moab and almost didn't make it back. If it weren't for God's intervening and ending the famine, perhaps Naomi never would have returned. And if it weren't for Ruth's determination to follow Naomi to Bethlehem, she never would have met Boaz. And if she had not met Boaz … well, you get the idea. The point is that a whole lot of unlikely things happened before we get "Jesse of Bethlehem."

> **With Jesse's heritage in mind, keep reading 1 Samuel 16:2-13.**
>
> **Which son did Samuel hastily think was the Lord's anointed, and why does Scripture suggest he thought so (vv. 6-7)?**

The Book of Ruth ends with a genealogy that ties Ruth, Boaz, and Naomi's smaller story into the much greater one … our own stories too are part of a divine whole.

Finish writing Yahweh's response to Samuel in verse 7 (NIV): "The LORD does not …"

Circle the word that appears four times.

I think it's interesting that Samuel, one of the godliest men of his day, fell prey to judging by outward appearance. Height, stature, a royal physique—Samuel thought he knew what a king looked like. But the Lord knew that the true measure of a king could only be determined from the inside. And only God has the vision to do this perfectly.

Personal Response: How do you fall into the faulty mind-set of judging by outward appearance (even if it's in judging yourself)?

Only God looks on the heart perfectly.

A friend of mine just called me in tears over a false accusation by someone important to her. I was literally putting the finishing touches on today's study, and my Bible was open to 1 Samuel 16 when the phone rang. First I listened. And then I reminded her that only God looks on the heart perfectly and that He sees her innocence.

Personal Response: Have you ever been in a situation where you were unjustly judged? Are you in one now? How can you take comfort in knowing that God can truly see your heart?

The Bible speaks prolifically about the heart. Here are a few of my favorites.

1. Read Deuteronomy 8:2. How did God test the hearts of the Israelites?

2. Read Proverbs 4:23. What are we to do with our hearts?

3. Read Hebrews 10:22. Because of Jesus, how does God allow us to draw near to Him?

Hebrews 10:22
Let us draw near to God with a sincere heart in full assurance of faith, having our hearts sprinkled to cleanse us from a guilty conscience and having our bodies washed with pure water.

Turn back to 1 Samuel 16. Whom did the Lord tell Samuel to anoint, and from where did his family have to retrieve him?

I can't help but note the similarities between David and his great-grandmother, Ruth: David was brought in from a humble field and Ruth was gathered from a foreign land. Both were unlikely choices to carry on the royal line of Judah, and both needed someone greater and more powerful than themselves to see them—not just their outward appeal but the richness and purity of their hearts. Such sight takes a special vision.

Turn back to Ruth and read 2:11 and 3:11. Just like the Lord chose David because of his heart, why was Boaz drawn to Ruth?

First Samuel 16:12 says that David had a ruddy glow and a fine appearance with handsome features. He was a good-looking guy who may have had Boaz's smile, Ruth's eyes, and Naomi's feisty red hair. But no matter what distinct features hung on through the generations, we know that in the same way the heart of Ruth drew the eyes of Boaz, so the heart of David drew the eyes of the Lord.

"For the eyes of the LORD range throughout the earth to show Himself strong for those whose hearts are completely His" (2 Chron. 16:9, HCSB).

Personal Response: Today's study is so personal that I don't want to specifically direct you. Close by responding to God however you feel moved.

DAY 04 LEGACY
RAHAB

I'm overlooking Boston Harbor on a pristinely cool and clear summer day, which my cab driver last night told me they'd only get approximately 11 more of this season, so I'm feeling even better about the cheery weather. He was a Nigerian cabbie in a Red Sox cap and I was in the back with a friend and a chocolate chip cannoli, all of which ministers to me on myriad levels. He was abnormally talkative and intent on fully turning around for feedback and gesturing, all with the normal fast-braking, swerving, and gas-pedal surging that cab drivers are known for. I mind this less when they're facing forward.

He told us that he'd started late that evening because his wife, Bobbie, was in the hospital with a mysterious infection and pneumonia. With unique expression he said that this caused him to have a "divided mind" while driving the city streets. I don't remember what got him started describing her, but you could tell through the veil of his broken English that he wanted us to understand who his wife was. "Do you know when people say 'someone is godly'? Well, my wife is godly!"

He went on to tell us how involved she is in her church, how she's always serving, and how at Christmastime she makes him drive her all around Boston to give out presents to the homeless. My friend and I almost burst into tears—and for reasons other than the homemade cannoli (which was so good it had made me tear up earlier). He told us that Bobbie studied zoology and got her masters in microbiology—a sharp woman, indeed—but when it all came down to it, he had one word to describe her: *godly*. I didn't get the impression he shared her faith, but how he admired her for it!

As we wound through Boston Commons, which literally cascades with legacy, I thought about Bobbie's life, how she was impacting the city, and how she was leaving her own legacy. And I thought about how blessed I would be if the one word someone used to describe me was *godly*. When we arrived at our hotel, we told our cab driver we'd be honored to pray for Bobbie to get out of that hospital bed—she obviously had a lot to get back to. I hope to meet her someday.

Personal Response: Who is someone you would describe as godly, and how has he or she impacted your life?

Though we will continue to look at genealogies today, I want to remind you that childbearing is not the only way to leave a legacy. Countless men and women who have never had children have impacted generations to come in unparalleled ways. The central ingredient to a divine legacy is godliness: to know God, to walk in His ways, and to teach future generations about who He is.

> Turn to Matthew 1:2-6. You'll notice the genealogy found in Ruth included in these verses.

> Starting in verse 3, compare Matthew's genealogy with Ruth's (4:18-22). What three additional names did Matthew give (besides Zerah)?

It was not Jewish custom to mention women in genealogies, especially not in a royal one, which is probably why we don't see any women listed in Ruth's genealogy. This sets Matthew apart who, as a Jew, willingly placed prominent women in his genealogy that began with Abraham, Isaac, and Jacob. This may not seem like a significant move in a day when women run for president or sit on the Supreme Court, but in Jewish culture this was a bold insertion.

> We've read about Tamar and Ruth, but how does Rahab fit into our study?

Boaz has been far too important for us to miss being introduced to his mother.* I mean, I'm curious to know who raised this exceptional man. What were her values, strengths, and did she cook with a lot of barley? The good news is that we can find some of this out in the Book of Joshua. See how much fun genealogies can be?

For instance, I'm sitting in the prestigious Boston Library where a man across from me just sat down and pulled out of his backpack a computer and a stuffed raccoon. He placed the raccoon on the table facing him, and it stared at him the whole time he studied. It was

The central ingredient to a divine legacy is godliness: to know God, to walk in His ways, and to teach future generations about who He is.

wearing a collar. See, this makes me want to know who his parents are, who his kids are, and whether or not I need my own raccoon.

Read Joshua 2:1-24 to learn about Rahab. (The setting is when Joshua sent spies into the land of Canaan to explore it before the Israelites attacked.)

What line of work was Rahab in?

What did Rahab do to help the Israelite spies?

How did Rahab know the Israelites served the one true God, since she was a Canaanite foreigner (vv. 8-11)?

What signal did Rahab have to give to be spared by the Israelites when they attacked Canaan (vv. 17-18)?

put blood over her door   tie a scarlet cord in her window

light a fire in her yard   open all her windows

Personal Take: What impacts you the most about this story, especially since she was the presumed mother of Boaz?

Read Joshua 6:15-17,22-25 to learn the outcome of Rahab's devotion to the spies. Then fill in the blank:

"And she [Rahab] lives among the _____ to this day" (v. 25). How is this similar to Ruth's story in Ruth 1:15-17?

Rahab was more than culturally distant from Israel; she was a prostitute.

Is this not amazing? The mother of Boaz was an outsider, a foreigner— the stuff we're used to with Ruth. But Rahab was more than culturally distant from Israel; she was a prostitute. But this is not the amazing part. The amazing part is that she came to live among the Israelites, made her home among God's people, married a man named Salmon, and eventually bore a son named Boaz. And not just any son, but a son King David would one day call his great-grandfather. This is the gospel.

To all the women whose pasts are sullied, this is the gospel. To those who are sure they have nothing to offer, this is the gospel. To those who never thought they could live among God's church, this is the gospel. For the woman who's afraid her life cannot be spared, that she's only as good as her body, that it's too late to undo the damage, this is the gospel.

Personal Response: How does Rahab's story of coming to live among God's people speak to your own story? Be specific.

In closing, read Hebrews 11:31. What did the writer of Hebrews say Rahab did by faith?

While meeting with the girls last week, Alli mentioned Rahab's unique story in connection with Boaz. She got me thinking along the lines of how Rahab's Canaanite (foreign) heritage might have played into Boaz's gutsy redemption of Ruth.

For Discussion: How may Rahab's story have influenced Boaz's compassion for Ruth?

Personal Response: Spend some time praying that God would give you eyes to see the outsider. That your prejudices would be dismantled. That you would learn to look on the heart, as we learned yesterday is so precious to God.

*Author's Note: It is possible that Salmon and Rahab were not Boaz's parents, but perhaps grandparents, great-grandparents or even further removed. This is because in biblical genealogies generations can be skipped in between mentions of names (though we don't know this is the case here). Either way, Boaz would have been very familiar with Rahab and her story since family history was vital to Jewish people.

DAY 05 LEGACY
A SAVIOR IS BORN

I realize that in this moment I am tying up one of the more memorable projects of my life. I'll never get to do this again—not exactly this. Write another Bible study, I hope, but write about a Moabitess who loved the God of Israel, who packed up her belongings to take care of a woman who wasn't blood and who didn't want her, who risked her life in the fields, who risked her life on the threshing floor, who drew the eyes of a noble man, married him, bore a son, and then placed the baby on the breast of the mother in-law she so desperately loved. Ruth. It will forever be my privilege to have written about her.

And then there is the other great privilege of sharing this journey with you—getting to add my thoughts and passions to the pages of Scripture you've so purposefully studied. I only wish I got to hear more of your own insights, how Naomi, Ruth, Boaz and God have changed your life, what you discussed with one another in your own living rooms, churches, or favorite cafes over coffee and tea, perhaps with restless children running around. What recipes were your favorites, what moments of prayer the most penetrating. And if anyone decided that entrusting her life to God was infinitely worth it after all.

Thank you. Thank you for this honor.

I have saved this day for last, not only because it naturally falls at the end but because it is the crown of our story. Yesterday we focused on the names from Ruth's genealogy as recorded in the Gospel of Matthew. We read the names that came before it, such as Abraham, Isaac, and Jacob, and noticed some extra women, Tamar, Ruth, and Rahab, who had been noticeably added. But today we will look at a name that comes after King David, where the Book of Ruth leaves off— the name that is above all names.

Yesterday we read from Matthew 1:2, but today I want you to start at the top.

> **Read Matthew 1:1-16. According to verse 1, whose genealogy is this a record of and who is announced in verse 16?**

The Scriptures foretold long ago that the promised Messiah, Jesus Christ, would come from Bethlehem and would arise as a ruler from King David's family.

Read Isaiah 11:1-5,10. From whose "stump" would Christ shoot?

According to Micah 5:2-5, from what city would this great Ruler of Israel come?

Perhaps one of the most famous passages foretelling the birth of Christ is Isaiah 9:6-7. On whose throne would He sit?

Personal Take: Turn back to Ruth and read 1:11-14. How does our understanding of Ruth's place in the line of Christ make the verses you just read more significant than ever before?

I don't understand how God's sovereignty works, like what would have happened if Ruth had followed Orpah back to Moab; if she hadn't pressed forth with determination to make the God of Israel her God, no matter the cost; if she'd succumbed to Naomi's reasoning—*she's right, I'll never find a husband in Bethlehem*. I don't know how Obed would have been born, or Jesse, or David, or Joseph, or what this would have done to the line from which Jesus came. I can't harness this mystery, all I know is that I'm glad Ruth didn't turn back, that she stayed the course. Her example inspires me to do the same.

Personal Response: How does the notion of Ruth's unwavering commitment to God—and the astounding ramifications— encourage you to remain faithful in difficult times?

I presume we have no idea how the biggest and seemingly insignificant decisions affect our lives and those around us. This doesn't mean we

> We have no idea how our decisions affect our lives and those around us.

need to obsess and overanalyze and drive ourselves nuts, wondering if we should have bought that orange from the other vendor around the corner or taken the highway instead of the back roads today. It only means we have to pursue Christ. He works all the other things out.

Personal Response: As you ponder the past six weeks, what is the single most impacting moment you had during this study?

I am personally amazed at how God masterfully preserved the line of Judah so many times over by the fragile threads of foreigners like Ruth, heartbroken widows like Naomi, deceptive affairs like Tamar's, prostitutes like Rahab, seduced women like Bathsheba, and humble teenagers like Mary. Only the gospel can make sense of such things.

> I hope you leave this study with a fuller, deeper, and more supreme grasp of the good news of the gospel: the *hesed* of Jesus Christ.

If there is anything I hope you will leave this study with, it is a fuller, deeper, and more supreme grasp of the good news of the gospel: The *hesed* of Jesus Christ—"the consistent, ever-faithful, relentless, constantly-pursuing, lavish, extravagant, unrestrained, covenant, furious love"—given to us.[1] Boaz beautifully demonstrated it to Ruth, Ruth lavishly bestowed it upon Naomi, and even Naomi grew in *hesed* for Ruth. From all of these imperfect and unlikely intertwining relationships came a Son … a Savior, from the town of David, who would take away the sins of the world. Absolutely amazing.

Personal Response: Meditate on the verses below and close with a prayer of thanksgiving for our magnificent redemption.

"He has raised up a horn of salvation for us in the house of his servant David" (Luke 1:69).

"Today in the town of David a Savior has been born to you; he is Christ the Lord" (Luke 2:11).

"The shepherds said to one another, 'Let's go to Bethlehem and see this thing that has happened, which the Lord has told us about' " (Luke 2:15).

"For my eyes have seen your salvation, which you have prepared in the sight of all people, a light for revelation to the Gentiles and for the glory of your people Israel" (Luke 2:30-32).

LOSS, LOVE & LEGACY

Paul Buono & Kelly Minter
See the story behind the song at www.livingroomseries.com.

Got my head turned round looking back
Lots of winding roads and dead end tracks
Surprising faces and distant lands
Don't know how I got here but here I am

Chorus
Life is loss, love and legacy
It's heartache and mystery
It's holding on when nothing makes sense
To find the crown when you reach the end

Shattered pieces and broken dreams
Picked up and put back by hands unseen
Beauty and blessing rise out of the ash
Raining down on me now that the rain is past

Chorus

Bridge
Every wound and every secret, every joy and victory
Woven altogether our Redeemer Redeems

Kelly Minter & Paul Buono. MintyFresh Music (ASCAP)/Pollen Days Publishing (BMI)

To purchase this song or CD go to
www.LifeWay.com/livingroomseries.

SOUTHWEST CHICKEN SOUP
SERVES 6

This is an easy favorite that's both quick and delicious. Extra good during football season.

12 oz. salsa verde (or make your own!)
3 cups cooked chicken (you can use an oven roasted chicken from your grocery to save time, or you can use the whole chicken recipe on p. 88)
15 oz. cannellini beans, drained
3 cups chicken broth (You can use canned broth for a soupier mixture.)
1 teaspoon ground cumin (I use more!)
1 package frozen corn
chili powder to taste
2 green onions, chopped
sour cream
tortilla chips

Directions
Empty salsa into a large sauce pan. Heat 2 minutes over medium high heat. Then add chicken, beans, broth, cumin, corn, and chili powder. Bring to a boil; lower heat to simmer 10 minutes, stirring occasionally.

Top each serving with onions, sour cream, and chips.

MOM'S CORNBREAD
PRE-HEAT OVEN TO 400° SERVES 6-8

This goes great opposite the Southwest Chicken Soup, and it's as easy as pie … or cornbread.

1 cup self-rising corn meal
¾ cup milk
1 egg
1 tablespoon oil

Directions
Stir ingredients together in a mixing bowl. Pour into a greased 8x8" pan and bake at 400° for 20 minutes or until brown.

Double recipe for a 9x13" pan.

Ruth: Loss, Love & Legacy is a discussion-based Bible study promoting honest conversation and relationships as women study Scripture together. Since conversation is essential to the experience, I've written a few starter questions to help get the discussion rolling each week. (Note: These questions are in addition to the "For Discussion" questions that appear frequently throughout the book.) You may not need the catalysts if your group is talkative and knows where it wants to go, but if ever you hit a lull, they can be referenced. As your group gets increasingly more comfortable with one another, you may find yourself needing these questions less. My ultimate hope is that each group will have its own Scriptures, principles, truths, experiences, and life stories that will naturally feed the conversation each week.

As you converse with one another, remember that digging deep into your own life and sharing with your group will help you grow in relationship. I've always been really encouraged when one of the "Nogs" (Alli, Lauri, Carrie ,and Anadara) has been brave enough to share something personal—it makes me feel not as alone in my own struggles and questions. Also note that different ages, backgrounds, stages of life, or races will only make your conversation and experience all the richer, so don't be afraid to share based on differences you perceive in your group. I love nothing more than to hear from older women when I have the opportunity, and I am just now discovering that they seem to appreciate my insight as well. This is a real gift if you have the opportunity for a diverse group. That's not to say that doing a Bible study with some of your best friends isn't a great idea as well. There's a lot of flexibility here.

If you can eat together and still keep your group small, you'll likely genuinely share with one another. The more intimate environment will allow you to honestly express your hearts in a way you might not in a more formal or larger setting. This also promotes specific and intimate times of prayer. However, many people have used the *The Living Room Series* studies in large groups that have been effective as well. This study can easily translate into a church small group or larger Sunday School setting, especially if your teacher would enjoy teaching the study. But, hey, so far we've heard of people meeting at Starbucks®, swim practice, the park, large church settings, so whatever fits your need. We add recipes to encourage groups to eat together because so many great friendships and conversations naturally start around a dinner table. However, these are merely suggestions. Feel free to use *Ruth* however you find is best for your group.

Because this study is discussion-based rather than leader-based, it is essential that all women feel comfortable sharing. It's not necessary to have a specific leader for Ruth; however, you may want to have one woman look over the questions in advance each week, think about a direction and prepare if anything needs to be done. Sharing the cooking and hosting responsibilities is always a good idea as well, unless one person is up for the task each week. You can decide.

I hope this helps. Please remember the Web site *www.lifeway.com/livingroomseries* for more help plus fun video clips with the "Nogs." More than anything, just remember to be real with one another, pray often, and enjoy the study of such a remarkable book in Scripture.

01 TWO JOURNEYS

1. What drew you to studying the Book of Ruth? What's one thing you hope to receive from it over the next six weeks?

2. What was the most impacting moment for you this week? (Bible verse, principle, prayer experience, revelation, new understanding, conviction, or other)

3. Discuss a time in your life when you were tempted to leave the place God had you in for something easier or more attractive (think about Elimilech and Naomi leaving the land of Bethlehem for Moab).

4. Read aloud Psalm 16:5-6 from day 2. Discuss the ways you can see these verses played out in your life. And if it's not as clear to you, be honest with that.

5. How does your heart go out to Naomi, Orpah, and Ruth? How has the devastation or hardship in your own life affected (good or bad) your relationship with Christ?

6. How has the word *hesed* enriched your understanding of love (day 3)?

7. Has a certain hardship in your life caused you turn around in your weeping or to weep going forward? Discuss.

8. What's an area in your life where you've had to choose a long obedience in the same direction (day 4)?

9. Discuss what you learned about the power of words (day 5).

10. How does Ruth's loyalty to Naomi encourage you to show this same type of committed loyalty to a friend or loved one who might not always be the easiest to love?

MENU

CHICKEN ENCHILADAS
MEXICAN ICE CREAM SUNDAE

PLAYLIST

01 THE DAY OF SMALL THINGS
by Alli Rogers on *The Day of Small Things*
Ruth never despised the small. She humbled herself for any task.
www.allirogers.com

02 YOU NEVER LET GO
by Matt Redman on *Beautiful News*
Through Naomi and Ruth's tragedy God never let them go.
www.mattredman.com

03 GO
by Anadara on *Into the Unknown*
Our journeys are taken by faith; Ruth didn't know where she was going but knew she had to go.
www.anadara.com

02 ARRIVING

1. Where was the last place you were ecstatic to arrive? (doesn't have to be a physical place)

2. In what areas have you been angry with or disappointed in God? Were you honest with Him this week (day 1)?

3. Have someone read Psalm 126:1-6 for the group. How does this psalm encourage you to keep sowing in the middle of difficult times, and how can you practically do this?

4. Ruth was a Moabitess in Israel. What experiences or family history make you feel less accepted in God's family (day 3)?

5. How does Boaz's kindness toward Ruth affect you? (If you're single, have you given up on finding a good man? If married, do his strengths remind you of your husband's?)

6. What did you learn about God's providence this week, and how does this help you rest in life's whacky circumstances? Share examples of God's providence in your life (day 3).

7. Discuss Ruth's work ethic and how it played into God's blessing her. How can you be a more diligent worker? Or if you overwork, how can you more purposefully rest?

8. How did Boaz's kindness to Ruth encourage you to show extravagant kindness to others? I really hope you can discuss specific ways of showing kindness to the poor and vulnerable around you—even the difficult to love.

9. Discuss Ruth's character and how it is making a name for her. How do we make names for ourselves—through our character and integrity or through other less important things such as materialism?

10. What stood out to you the most this week—something that really made you think?

MENU

FRESH TOMATO PASTA
PARMESAN FLAT BREAD

PLAYLIST

01 I NEED A SAVIOR
by Anadara on *A Little Closer*
Makes me think of Ruth walking through the gates of Bethlehem seeking her Savior.
www.anadara.com

....

02 I WILL SAY
by Lou Fellingham on *Treasure*
One of my favorite songs from one of my favorite worship leaders. How Ruth patiently waited for her redemption to come!
www.loufellingham.com

....

03 THE GRATEFUL
by Tim Timmons on *The Grateful*
After all the hardship, Ruth had begun to experience blessing. It's good to stop and be grateful.
www.timmonsmusic.com

03 AN ENCOUNTER

1. What did you think of Lisa's story and the kindness of the probation officer in the introduction to week 3? Did it encourage you to be kind to others in the little things?

2. Read Isaiah 58:6-12 aloud. How does this encourage you to show kindness, self-sacrifice, and loyalty to those in need, especially to your family?

3. How have you found shelter under the wings of the Lord? Share specific examples with one another to help encourage each other's faith.

4. Discuss humility (day 2). How did this impact you?

5. In what area of your life is showing humility specifically challenging for you?

6. After reading about Ruth and Mephibosheth's invitation to the table, how did this help you more deeply appreciate your own invitation to the wedding feast of the Lamb? If this is a new concept for you, feel free to discuss your questions and feelings in your group (day 3).

7. Are you in a season of reaping, sowing, or both? Discuss specifically with each other.

8. In what ways can you be generous in your season of sowing or harvesting?

9. On day 5 we learned Naomi and Ruth had not been left without a kinsman-redeemer, reminding us that God has not left us without Christ, our Kinsman-Redeemer. How does the picture of Naomi and Ruth make you further appreciate that God has not left us without a Redeemer?

10. What piece of information about a kinsman-redeemer meant the most to you and why (especially as it relates to Christ as our Kinsman-Redeemer) (day 5)?

MENU

GRILLED CHICKEN SALAD WITH STRAWBERRIES
BANOFFI PIE

PLAYLIST

01 GOD OF JUSTICE
by Tim Hughes on *Happy Day—Live*
Reminds me of how Boaz redeemed Ruth and how we are called to extend ourselves to the poor.
www.timhughesmusic.com

02 BEHOLD THE LAMB
by Stuart Townend on *There Is a Hope*
I love leading this song at communion. Makes me think of Boaz inviting Ruth to his table and God inviting us to His.
www.stuarttownend.co.uk

03 PSALM 62
by Aaron Keyes on *Not Guilty Anymore*
Ruth found refuge under the wings of God who was her ultimate delight and reward.
www.aaronkeyes.com

04 A PROPOSAL

1. I talked about what has drawn me to Ruth. What about her or her story has drawn you the most?

2. If you were Ruth on your way to the threshing floor, what part of the process would have required the most courage?

3. If you feel comfortable, share about a time in your life when you've taken off your "clothes of mourning" and moved forward in obedience.

4. Did this week open your eyes to anything you've been clinging to that has been holding you back (bitterness, unforgiveness, anger, disappointment, hopelessness)?

5. In day 3 we read about Ruth lying down at Boaz's feet. How have you been able to do this successfully, and what has hindered you or stood in your way?

6. Ruth's proposal to Boaz was unique. If you're married, share how your husband (or you) proposed. If you're single, share how you hope it might happen. Speaking as a single woman myself, hoping and dreaming is good—so don't feel embarrassed by talking about your loftiest hope.

7. What's your reaction to the nearer relative who could have redeemed Naomi's property and inherit Ruth—but didn't? Have you ever felt capable in a situation but unwilling?

8. Ruth had to wait through the night for an answer. What have you learned about waiting this week?

9. Discuss the principle of Christ being our supply of what we're to deliver and lavish on others (day 5). How does this relieve you of carrying everyone else's burdens?

10. How did the romance between Boaz and Ruth stir your heart this week? Does it make you long for romance? Does it give you a gratefulness for the romance you have?

MENU

CURRY CHICKEN
CHICK-PEA AND DRIED FRUIT COUSCOUS
MOM'S ICE CREAM DESSERT

PLAYLIST

01 COME NOW MY LOVE
by Alli Rogers on *You and the Evening Sky*
Ruth became the bride of Boaz. We have become the bride of Christ.
www.allirogers.com

02 JESUS DRAW ME EVER NEARER
by Margaret Becker on *New Irish Hymns*
Ruth had to wait through the dark passage of night, but she was drawn ever nearer to God.
www.maggieb.com

03 NEW DAY
by Robbie Seay Band on *Give Yourself Away*
Love this when I think of Ruth flinging off her widow's clothes. Baby, it's a new day!
www.robbieseayband.com

05 REDEMPTION

1. How did Gloria's story of starting "Ray of Hope" encourage you to step out in your faith?

2. Discuss how this week's study has opened your eyes to looking for the "Ruths" God has placed in your life.

3. If you feel comfortable sharing, where are you in the process of totally surrendering your life to the Lord? Are you holding certain things back? Are certain things scarier for you to offer Him than others? This will be encouraging if a few people share about this one.

4. What do you think of being willing to be made willing?

5. How did studying Christ's willingness to redeem you further impact your understanding of His love for you?

6. How did Boaz's proclamation of redeeming "Ruth the Moabitess, Mahlon's widow" in Ruth 4:10 impact you when you think of how Christ has redeemed us personally—with all our baggage, sin, mired pasts, and imperfections?

7. On day 4 we looked at the idea of blessing. If you're up for it, consider having each person in the group share a biblical blessing over the person to her right or left.

8. Discuss your thoughts about Rachel and Leah's story and Tamar's story. Did this give you a greater understanding of how Ruth fits into the bigger picture of Scripture?

9. In session 4 we talked about Boaz sacrificing to carry on Elimilech's name. How have you laid down your life for someone else (child, parent, friend, spouse, etc.)?

10. As women, what did the marriage of Boaz and Ruth and the blessing of a son stir up in you (good or bad)? Did it give you hope or make you sad? Discuss your reaction with one another.

MENU

CLASSIC LASAGNA WITH HOMEMADE NOODLES
INSALATA ESTIVA

PLAYLIST

01 IF I'M BRAVE
by Alli Rogers
Reminds me of Ruth heading to the threshing floor. Walking brave.
www.allirogers.com

02 BUILD THIS HOUSE
by Lou Fellingham on *Build This House*
The women prayed that Ruth would build up the house of Israel. "Unless the LORD builds the house, its builders labor in vain." Psalm 127:1
www.loufellingham.com

03 I KNOW THAT MY REDEEMER LIVES
by Chris McClarney from *Revive (Live Worship)*
Long after Ruth and Boaz, Christ was born, our Redeemer. You'll love this old hymn redone and led by an amazing singer and worship leader, Chris McClarney.

06 LEGACY

1. What will you miss the most about studying the Book of Ruth with one another?

2. Discuss your reaction to Naomi being celebrated with Obed at the end of the book. Do you think this is right, good, fair?

3. At the end of day 1 (p. 147) I wrote: "But grace stuns our theories and carefully constructed notions of how things should go. It blesses those who don't deserve it, redeems names that would otherwise have disappeared, and sets glory in the bosoms of once-forsaken widows." How has grace "stunned you"?

4. In what ways are you leaving a legacy? Has studying Ruth and Boaz's life helped you better understand its importance, even if it's not through actual childbearing?

5. Has someone recently refreshed your life as Obed refreshed and renewed Naomi's?

6. Were you surprised to see that Ruth was the great-great-grandmother of King David? How did this add to the richness of Ruth and Boaz's story for you?

7. What was your reaction to Rahab's story? Does it surprise you that so many marred women showed up in the genealogy of Jesus Christ? How does this encourage you?

8. How did studying the genealogy in Ruth and Matthew help you further understand how Scripture ties together? Was this intriguing to you?

9. We studied this week Old Testament prophecies that point toward Christ. How did they strengthen your faith?

10. What was the single most impacting part of this study for you?

MENU

SOUTHWEST CHICKEN SOUP
MOM'S CORNBREAD

PLAYLIST

01 WHAT I DO WITH YOUR TIME
by Anadara on *A Little Closer*
Leaving a legacy is inextricably linked to what we do with the time God's given us here.
www.anadara.com

....

02 LEGACY
by Nichole Nordeman on *Double Take: Nichole Nordeman*
The title sums it up.
www.nicholenordeman.com

....

03 SONG OF THE BEAUTIFUL
by Christy Nockels on *Life Light Up*
At the end of it all, this is our song: Jesus loves us.
www.christynockels.com

ENDNOTES

Week 1

1. Matthew Henry, *Matthew Henry's Commentary on the Whole Bible,* Vol. 2. [Cited 7 July 2009]. Available from the Internet: *www.ccel.org/ccel/henry/mhc2.viii.ii.html*
2. Ibid.
3. Warren W.Wiersbe, *The Bible Exposition Commentary, OT History* (Colorado Springs, CO: Cook Communications Ministries, 2003), 180.
4. Daniel I. Block, "Judges, Ruth" in *The New American Commentary* (Nashville, TN: Broadman & Holman Publishers, 1999), 605.
5. Robert L. Hubbard, Jr., *The Book of Ruth* (Grand Rapids, MI: William B. Eerdmans Publishing Company, 1988), 104.
6. Iain M. Duguid, *Esther and Ruth* (Phillipsburg, NJ: P&R Publishing Co., 2005), 163.
7. Wiersbe, 181.
8. Charley McMaster Bondurant quoting Frederich Nietzsche. [Cited 7 July 2009]. Available from the Internet: *www.spiritrestoration.org/bookreviews/A%20Long%20Obedience%20in%20The%20Same%20Direction.htm quote*

Week 2

1. Hubbard, 123.
2. Tim Keller, *Genesis Study* (Copyright Timothy J. Keller and Redeemer Presbyterian Church, 2008), 118.
3. Hubbard, 131.
4. Block, 651.
5. Block, 653.
6. Elizabeth Barrett Browning [Cited 9 July 2009]. Available from the *Internet: http://thinkexist.com/quotation/earth-s_crammed_with_heaven-and_every_common_bush/205499.html*
7. Hubbard, 160.
8. Block, 660.
9. Ibid.

Week 3

1. Block, 671.
2. Block, 673.
3. Hubbard, 188.
4. Block, 674-675.
5. Hubbard, 674.

Week 4

1. Block, 684.
2. Block, 690.
3. "Joshua, Judges, Ruth" in *Ancient Christian Commentary on Scripture.* Edited by John R. Franke. (Downer's Grove, IL: InterVarsity Press, 2005), 187.
4. Duigid, 173.

Week 5

1. Lucy Maud Montgomery, *Anne of Green Gables.* [Cited 21 July 2009]. Available from the Internet: *http://greengables-2.tripod.com/script/2part1.html*
2. Diguid, 182.
3. Block, 720.
4. Hubbard, 256-257.
5. Ibid., 267.

Week 6

1. *Hesed Interactive.* [2000] [Cited 23 July 2009]. Available from the Internet: *http://www.hesed.com/heseddef.htm*

Page 174 Gospel Explanation

1. Herbert Lockyer, *All The Women of The Bible,* 149.

THE GREATER STORY OF REDEMPTION

To see the Book of Ruth as a simple love story or an interesting chronicle is to miss its much grander story of redemption. This remarkable narrative goes far beyond the personal ventures of Ruth, Naomi, and Boaz; and if we don't grasp this we miss the most miraculous part of the story: The foreshadowing of our own redemption through Jesus Christ. He is our ultimate Kinsman-Redeemer, the One who came to save us from our own versions of Moab. Who came to save us from our sin.

The idea of being a sinner or in need of a Savior can seem antiquated and offensive, especially in our culture. But acknowledging our lostness before God is surprisingly liberating, first because it offers an explanation for the extreme brokenness we so often feel with God, with one another, and even with creation. Thankfully, this acknowledgment gives us far more than an explanation; it opens up our hearts to a Savior. And because broken sinners are the treasure of His eye ("For the Son of Man [Jesus] came to seek and to save the lost," Luke 19:10), suddenly we find ourselves in a surprisingly hopeful place.

Perhaps you have fared better than me, but I have made a terrible savior for myself. And when I have turned to other gods such as people, possessions, career paths, entertainment, and aesthetics, I have been miserably disappointed. I am freed by the truth that I cannot save myself and that there is no other God who can satisfy, because this is the entry point to experiencing the grace of Jesus. And because I just can't think of anything more awful than being my own god.

This is one of the primary things that sets Christianity apart from other major religions. Salvation does not depend on our moral goodness. There is nothing we can do to earn it; instead, it is a gift attained for us through Christ. This is depicted beautifully in the Book of Ruth in that Ruth had no standing on her own. She couldn't become an Israelite apart from Boaz's redemption of her. Even in her "goodness," she needed a redeemer to rescue her from the claims of Moab, invite her to his table, call her his own, restore her name, and give her a lasting legacy.

This is the beautiful offer Jesus extends to us that came at an infinite cost. He died on a cross, separated from God, so He could absorb the punishment that should have been ours. Someone had to bear the extreme destruction of our sin; and instead of us bearing it in endless separation from our Creator, the perfect Son of God stepped into our world and bore it for us. And after He died for our sin, He was raised from the dead so we could be saved by His life (Rom. 5:10). Never has a Redeemer been closer.

Wherever you are in the Book of Ruth, my prayer is that you will not just see a noble man adoring and rescuing a remarkable woman, but that you will see your own story scripted throughout its pages. That you will know in the deepest recesses of your heart that a Savior, infinitely greater than Boaz, has seen you, sought you, given His very life for you, and invited you to His table. My hope is that you will revel in the freeness (not cheapness) of the linens of forgiveness that Jesus offers and that you will receive the invitation of eternal life, which is to know Jesus, the only true God (John 17:3). It is then that you will truly understand what the Book of Ruth is all about.

> "In the soul of Jesus the wedding bells of Ruth and Boaz are rung once more. Here again Moab and Israel meet together. In the heart of the Son of Man the Gentile stands side by side with the Jew as the recipient of a common divine fatherhood."[1]

Contact us at *info@livingroomseries.com* if you have further thoughts or questions.